Volume IV
Postwar Prosperity and the Cold War
(1946–1963)

The Twentieth Century

The Progressive Era and
the First World War
(1900–1918)

The Roaring Twenties and
an Unsettled Peace
(1919–1929)

The Great Depression
and World War II
(1930–1945)

Postwar Prosperity
and the Cold War
(1946–1963)

The Civil Rights Movement
and the Vietnam Era
(1964–1975)

Baby Boomers and the
New Conservatism
(1976–1991)

Volume IV
Postwar Prosperity and the Cold War
(1946-1963)

Editorial Consultants

Matthew T. Downey, University of California at Berkeley
Harvey Green, Northeastern University
David M. Katzman, University of Kansas
Ruth Jacknow Markowitz, SUNY College at Oswego
Albert E. Moyer, Virginia Polytechnic Institute

Macmillan Publishing Company
New York
Maxwell Macmillan Canada
Toronto

Editorial Credits

Developed and produced by Visual Education Corporation,
Princeton, N.J.

Project Editor: Richard Bohlander

Associate Project Editor: Michael Gee

Writers: Linda Barrett, Cathie Cush, Galen Guengerich,
Lois Markham, Donna Singer

Editors: Risa Cottler, Susan Garver, Amy Lewis, Linda Scher,
Betty Shanley, Bonnie Swaim, Frances Wiser

Production Supervisor: Mary Lyn Sodano

Inputting: Cindy Feldner

Interior Design: Maxson Crandall

Cover Design: Mike McIver

Layout: Maxson Crandall, Lisa Evans, Graphic Typesetting
Service, Elizabeth Onorato

Photo Research: Cynthia Cappa, Sara Matthews

Maps: Parrot Graphics

Graphs: Virtual Media

Proofreading Management: Amy Davis

Photo Credits

AP/Wide World Photos: 3 (far right), 106

Archive Photos: 3 (3rd fom left), 62

Brown Brothers: 88, 98 (right)

© 1978 Robert Phillips/Black Star: 27

Ewing Galloway: 3 (5th from left), 14, 90

George C. Marshall Research Foundation: 40

J. R. Eyerman/Life Magazine © 1954 Time Warner Inc.: 97

Joe Munroe: 12 (bottom)

Leonard McCombe/Life Magazine © Time Warner Inc.: 12 (top)

Museum of The City of New York: 99

Photoworld/FPG International: 80

Rudolph Burckhardt: 105

Sovfoto: 84

Springer/Bettmann Film Archive: 116

The Bettmann Archive: 31, 41, 44, 49, 68, 76, 98 (left), 100

The National Archives: 3 (4th from left), 21, 42, 46, 78

UPI/Bettmann: 3 (2nd from left), 24, 36, 45, 50, 54, 55, 60, 72,
73, 82, 83, 85 (both), 86, 93, 101, 117 (left)

UPI/Bettmann Newsphotos: 3 (far left), 10, 16, 18, 26, 30, 34, 35,
57, 65, 67, 81, 87, 92, 95, 96, 108, 111, 112, 114, 115,
117 (right)

Macmillan Publishing Company
866 Third Avenue
New York, NY 10022

Maxwell Macmillan Canada, Inc.
1200 Eglinton Avenue East, Suite 200
Don Mills, Ontario M3C 3N1

Macmillan Publishing Company is part of the Maxwell
Communication Group of Companies

Printed in the United States of America

printing number
1 2 3 4 5 6 7 8 9 10

Library of Congress Cataloging-in-Publication Data

The twentieth century / consultants, Matthew T. Downey . . .
[et al.].
    p.   cm.
    Includes index.
    Contents: v. 1. The Progressive Era and the First World War
(1900–1918)—v. 2. The Roaring Twenties and an Unsettled
Peace (1919–1929)—v. 3. The Great Depression and World
War II (1930–1945)—v. 4. Postwar Prosperity and the Cold
War (1946–1963)—v. 5. The Civil Rights Movement and the
Vietnam Era (1964–1975)—v. 6. Baby Boomers and the New
Conservatism (1976–1991).
    ISBN 0-02-897442-5 (set : alk. paper)
    1. History, Modern—20th century. I. Downey, Matthew T.
D421.T88 1992
909.82—dc20   91-40862

Preface

The Twentieth Century is a six-book series covering the major developments of the period, from a primarily American perspective. This is the chronicle of a century unlike any before, one in which the pace of change has accelerated to the point that it is almost overwhelming.

As the century draws to a close, with such major ongoing events as the end of the Cold War and the seeming collapse of communism, it is appropriate to step back from the furious rush forward and examine the significance of the many changes we have seen in what may be the most momentous epoch in the history of the world.

Here, then, is the story of a world transformed by technology: by radio, television, and satellite communications; by automobiles, airplanes, and space travel; by antibiotics, organ transplants, and genetic engineering; by the atomic bomb; by the computer. These are just a few of the advances that have revolutionized the workings of the world and our daily lives.

Here also is the story of a century of history strongly influenced by individuals: Vladimir Lenin and Mao Ze-dong; Franklin Delano Roosevelt, Winston Churchill, and Adolf Hitler; Lech Walesa and Mikhail Gorbachev; Mohandas Gandhi and Martin Luther King Jr.; Theodore Roosevelt, John F. Kennedy, and Ronald Reagan. All have been featured actors in the drama of our times, as conveyed by these pages.

Above all else, it is the story of an American century, one in which a young democratic nation emerged as the world's most powerful force. Through two bitter world wars and an enduring cold war, the dominant influence of the United States on twentieth-century world history and culture is undeniable.

It is the story of the many forces that have transformed the face of our nation from a primarily rural, agricultural society dominated by white people of European heritage to a modern urban, industrialized, and multicultural nation. It is a story of the challenges, successes, and failures that have accompanied these fundamental changes.

Each book of this series focuses on a distinct era of the century. The six titles in the series are:

*The Progressive Era and
the First World War (1900–1918)*

*The Roaring Twenties and
an Unsettled Peace (1919–1929)*

*The Great Depression
and World War II (1930–1945)*

*Postwar Prosperity
and the Cold War (1946–1963)*

*The Civil Rights Movement
and the Vietnam Era (1964–1975)*

*Baby Boomers and the
New Conservatism (1976–1991)*

Each book is divided into six units: The Nation, The World, Business and Economy, Science and Technology, Arts and Entertainment, and Sports and Leisure. The second page of each unit includes a Datafile presenting significant statistical information in both table and graph format. All units include boxed features and sidebars focusing on particular topics of interest.

Additional features of each book include a graphic timeline of events of the period called Glimpses of the Era; a compilation of quotes, headlines, slogans, and literary extracts called Voices of the Era; a glossary of terms; a list of suggested readings; and a complete index.

The series is illustrated with historical photos, as well as original maps, graphs, and tables conveying pertinent statistical data.

Contents

GLIMPSES OF THE ERA

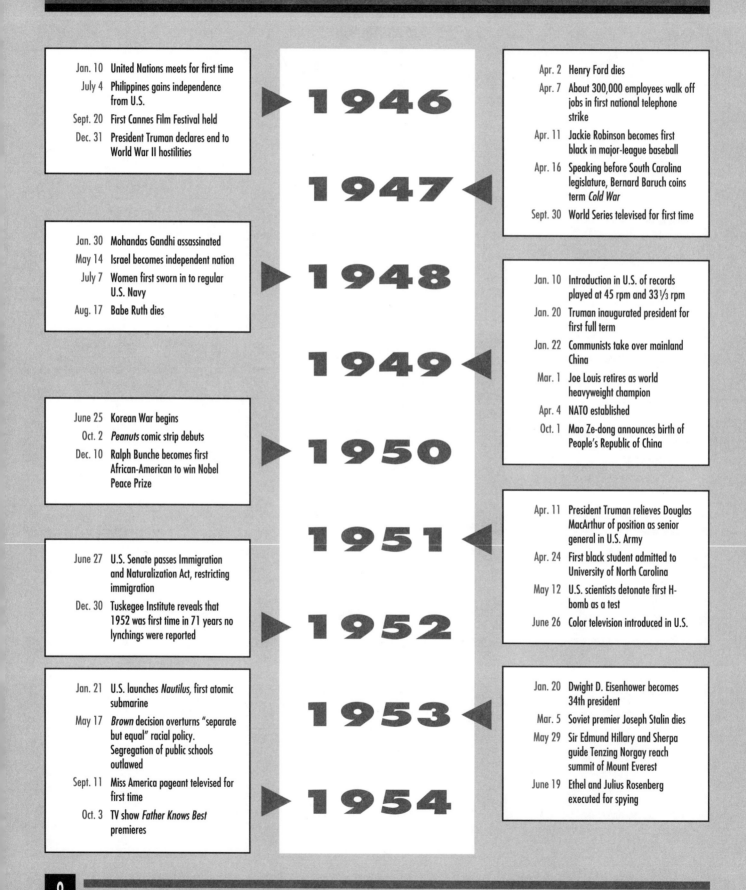

1946
- Jan. 10 — United Nations meets for first time
- July 4 — Philippines gains independence from U.S.
- Sept. 20 — First Cannes Film Festival held
- Dec. 31 — President Truman declares end to World War II hostilities

1947
- Apr. 2 — Henry Ford dies
- Apr. 7 — About 300,000 employees walk off jobs in first national telephone strike
- Apr. 11 — Jackie Robinson becomes first black in major-league baseball
- Apr. 16 — Speaking before South Carolina legislature, Bernard Baruch coins term *Cold War*
- Sept. 30 — World Series televised for first time

1948
- Jan. 30 — Mohandas Gandhi assassinated
- May 14 — Israel becomes independent nation
- July 7 — Women first sworn in to regular U.S. Navy
- Aug. 17 — Babe Ruth dies

1949
- Jan. 10 — Introduction in U.S. of records played at 45 rpm and 33⅓ rpm
- Jan. 20 — Truman inaugurated president for first full term
- Jan. 22 — Communists take over mainland China
- Mar. 1 — Joe Louis retires as world heavyweight champion
- Apr. 4 — NATO established
- Oct. 1 — Mao Ze-dong announces birth of People's Republic of China

1950
- June 25 — Korean War begins
- Oct. 2 — *Peanuts* comic strip debuts
- Dec. 10 — Ralph Bunche becomes first African-American to win Nobel Peace Prize

1951
- Apr. 11 — President Truman relieves Douglas MacArthur of position as senior general in U.S. Army
- Apr. 24 — First black student admitted to University of North Carolina
- May 12 — U.S. scientists detonate first H-bomb as a test
- June 26 — Color television introduced in U.S.

1952
- June 27 — U.S. Senate passes Immigration and Naturalization Act, restricting immigration
- Dec. 30 — Tuskegee Institute reveals that 1952 was first time in 71 years no lynchings were reported

1953
- Jan. 20 — Dwight D. Eisenhower becomes 34th president
- Mar. 5 — Soviet premier Joseph Stalin dies
- May 29 — Sir Edmund Hillary and Sherpa guide Tenzing Norgay reach summit of Mount Everest
- June 19 — Ethel and Julius Rosenberg executed for spying

1954
- Jan. 21 — U.S. launches *Nautilus,* first atomic submarine
- May 17 — *Brown* decision overturns "separate but equal" racial policy. Segregation of public schools outlawed
- Sept. 11 — Miss America pageant televised for first time
- Oct. 3 — TV show *Father Knows Best* premieres

GLIMPSES OF THE ERA

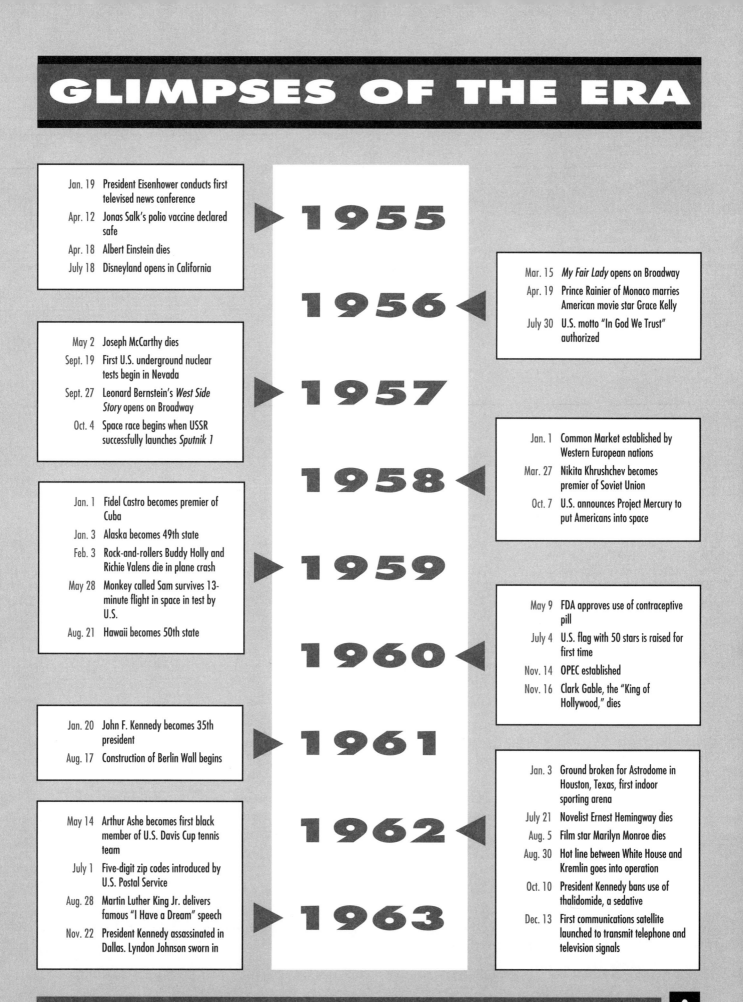

1955
- Jan. 19 President Eisenhower conducts first televised news conference
- Apr. 12 Jonas Salk's polio vaccine declared safe
- Apr. 18 Albert Einstein dies
- July 18 Disneyland opens in California

1956
- Mar. 15 *My Fair Lady* opens on Broadway
- Apr. 19 Prince Rainier of Monaco marries American movie star Grace Kelly
- July 30 U.S. motto "In God We Trust" authorized

1957
- May 2 Joseph McCarthy dies
- Sept. 19 First U.S. underground nuclear tests begin in Nevada
- Sept. 27 Leonard Bernstein's *West Side Story* opens on Broadway
- Oct. 4 Space race begins when USSR successfully launches *Sputnik 1*

1958
- Jan. 1 Common Market established by Western European nations
- Mar. 27 Nikita Khrushchev becomes premier of Soviet Union
- Oct. 7 U.S. announces Project Mercury to put Americans into space

1959
- Jan. 1 Fidel Castro becomes premier of Cuba
- Jan. 3 Alaska becomes 49th state
- Feb. 3 Rock-and-rollers Buddy Holly and Richie Valens die in plane crash
- May 28 Monkey called Sam survives 13-minute flight in space in test by U.S.
- Aug. 21 Hawaii becomes 50th state

1960
- May 9 FDA approves use of contraceptive pill
- July 4 U.S. flag with 50 stars is raised for first time
- Nov. 14 OPEC established
- Nov. 16 Clark Gable, the "King of Hollywood," dies

1961
- Jan. 20 John F. Kennedy becomes 35th president
- Aug. 17 Construction of Berlin Wall begins

1962
- Jan. 3 Ground broken for Astrodome in Houston, Texas, first indoor sporting arena
- July 21 Novelist Ernest Hemingway dies
- Aug. 5 Film star Marilyn Monroe dies
- Aug. 30 Hot line between White House and Kremlin goes into operation
- Oct. 10 President Kennedy bans use of thalidomide, a sedative
- Dec. 13 First communications satellite launched to transmit telephone and television signals

1963
- May 14 Arthur Ashe becomes first black member of U.S. Davis Cup tennis team
- July 1 Five-digit zip codes introduced by U.S. Postal Service
- Aug. 28 Martin Luther King Jr. delivers famous "I Have a Dream" speech
- Nov. 22 President Kennedy assassinated in Dallas. Lyndon Johnson sworn in

THE NATION

When Vice President Harry S. Truman entered the room on April 12, 1945, he sensed that something serious had happened. Mrs. Franklin Delano Roosevelt put her hand on his shoulder and said, "Harry, the president is dead." Within minutes, wire services had the news, and radio programs were interrupted: "We bring you a special bulletin . . ."

America was still at war. As the new president, Truman suddenly faced huge responsibilities. Then, on August 14, 1945, the war finally ended. Truman told a cheering crowd, "This is the day when fascism and police government cease in the world."

As millions of soldiers and sailors came back to their families, Americans wanted to get back to a normal peacetime life. While victory had made Americans proud of their country, they

AT A GLANCE

▶ Postwar America

▶ Politics After the New Deal

▶ The Chill in U.S.-Soviet Relations

▶ Cold War in America

▶ Blacks Battle for Equality

▶ The Promise of a New Frontier

feared a return to the depression that had put so many people out of work in the 1930s. The world war had changed the world in many ways, introducing new methods of mass destruction and an uncertain future even in its decisive conclusion.

Americans faced these worries on the threshold of a new era— one of rising prosperity, comfort, and mobility. For more and more people, normal life came to mean a home in the suburbs, a television in the living room, and cars in the garage. To ensure the security of their new lives, they turned to an ex-general, Dwight D. Eisenhower (above), to guide the nation. His eight years in office came to represent America's new pursuit of happiness amidst the powerful forces that were rapidly reshaping American society.

U.S. population	1950	1960
Total (in millions)	150.7	179.3
Urban	64.0%	70.0%
Rural	36.0%	30.0%
White	89.5%	88.6%
Black	10.0%	10.5%
Other	0.5%	0.9%

Social data	1946	1963
Birthrate (live births per 1,000 pop.)	24.1	21.7
Mortality rate (per 1,000 pop.)	10.0	9.6
Murder rate (per 100,000 pop.)	6.4	4.9
Persons ages 5–17 in school (per 100 pop.)	91.2	94.9

Voter turnout			
1948	53.0%	1956	60.6%
1952	63.3%	1960	64.0%

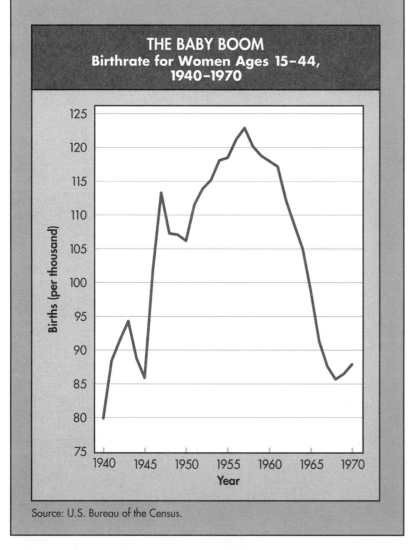

THE BABY BOOM
Birthrate for Women Ages 15–44, 1940–1970

Source: U.S. Bureau of the Census.

POSTWAR AMERICA

At the end of the war, more than 8 million American soldiers and sailors were eager to go home, but many were not sure what they were going home to. Millions of young adults like themselves would be looking for a job or an education and a place to live. Even as the government tried to control the flood of returning veterans, some 35,000 were discharged from the armed services each day in 1946. America had never experienced anything like this before.

The GI Bill

During the war, the government had made plans for the problems of returning to a peacetime economy. In 1944 Congress passed the Servicemen's Readjustment Act (called the "GI Bill") to help returning veterans adjust to civilian life. It gave them the right to return to a job they had held before the war, even though someone else might have taken their place during the war. The bill also extended job assistance and unemployment insurance to veterans. In total, the GI Bill was the largest government benefit program up to its time.

The GI Bill encouraged veterans to go to college or to continue their education if the war had interrupted it. Many more people enrolled in college, and new buildings and even new colleges were built to handle these new students. Because overcrowded colleges often had to use temporary housing for students and their families, some veterans found themselves living

► After World War II, ex-GIs received unemployment pay of $20 a week. The average veteran drew about two months' worth, though it could extend up to a year. This gave veterans plenty of time to think about their future.

again in military-style barracks. But most were glad for the chance to attend college at very little cost.

The GI Bill also allowed veterans to obtain low-interest loans, so they could afford to buy their own homes. At first, returning GIs were met by a severe housing shortage.

But armed with this buying power, their demand for homes sparked a huge boom in the housing market.

The Suburbs Take Shape

Victory abroad and raised expectations at home helped build optimism about America's place in the world, and also about its future. This outlook, and a pent-up desire for the good things in life, in turn fueled an economic boom, which began shortly after the war and continued into the next decade. Factories that had been making war machinery started making cars and household goods instead. Many jobs opened up for veterans and others. The housing boom provided many construction jobs. Work also became available in companies providing new goods and services and in new government jobs. Americans were enjoying a return to prosperity.

As veterans and others found that they could afford to buy their

► The pattern of almost identical houses in suburban Santa Clara, California, typified the new American landscape of the postwar era. Though they were sometimes built closely together, individual homes in the suburbs meant more space and privacy for families leaving the city.

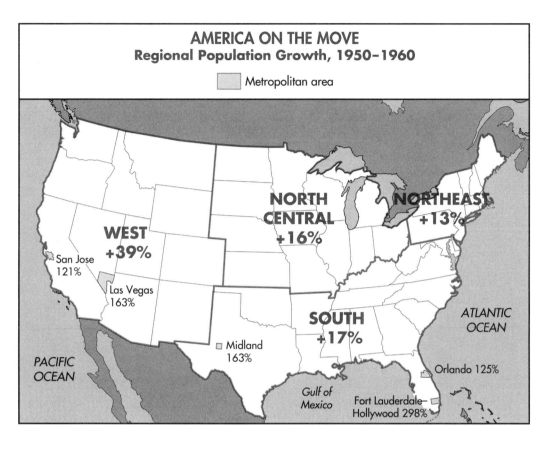

AMERICA ON THE MOVE
Regional Population Growth, 1950–1960

Metropolitan area

NORTHEAST +13%

NORTH CENTRAL +16%

WEST +39%

San Jose 121%

Las Vegas 163%

Midland 163%

SOUTH +17%

ATLANTIC OCEAN

PACIFIC OCEAN

Orlando 125%

Gulf of Mexico

Fort Lauderdale–Hollywood 298%

◀ The West grew more than twice as fast as any other region in the United States in the 1950s. The five fastest growing metropolitan areas—Fort Lauderdale-Hollywood, Las Vegas, Midland, Orlando, and San Jose—were spread across the Sunbelt.

own homes and start families, they often left the big cities and moved to the suburbs to live. Suburban growth was tremendous in the 1940s and 1950s. Areas outside of cities like Los Angeles, Houston, and New York grew at several times the rate of the cities themselves. To attract family-oriented buyers, builders created planned communities that included not only houses, but schools, parks, and shopping areas as well. Mass-produced developments, like Levittown, New York, sprang up, offering affordable homes. A house, a yard, and a garage were within reach of a wider range of middle-class families.

People left the cities behind for many reasons, not the least of which was the sense that a move to the suburbs was a move up in life. In addition to moderately priced housing, the suburbs offered new neighborhoods with all the modern facilities. There, families could enjoy spacious lawns and neighborhood parks without giving up many of the conveniences of city life. That more and more people were able to afford cars was a major factor in the growth of the suburbs. People could easily drive from their workplaces in the city to quieter, roomier locations in which to raise their families.

A Family Affair
Encouraged by all the signs of a booming economy, many young couples soon began having children. Birthrates soared following the war and throughout the 1950s, a period known as the Baby Boom. With more children, people needed bigger houses, more and better schools, and more places to play.

LITTLE BOXES
The spread of the suburbs in the 1950s attracted the attention of social critics, who observed the overwhelming sameness of suburban society. Because the suburbs drew mainly the same kind of people—white and middle-class—suburban culture reflected their values. Though these values were widely shared, critics noted the pressure that many suburban dwellers felt about looking and acting the same.

In a song called "Little Boxes," folksinger Malvina Reynolds made fun of suburban housing developments and their uniform houses. She went on to ridicule the bland conformity of the people who lived in the houses:

And the boys go into business
And marry and raise a family
In boxes made of ticky tacky
And they all look just the same.

Each day, millions of children start the school day by facing the American flag and reciting the Pledge of Allegiance, a promise of loyalty to the United States.

The oath, written in 1892 by Francis Bellamy, has been changed more than once. In 1924 the phrase "the flag of the United States of America" replaced the words "my flag." In 1954 President Eisenhower insisted that the phrase "under God" be added.

▼ The family of four barbecuing in the backyard became an icon of middle-class suburban life in the 1950s.

So the Baby Boom produced another boom in housing and school construction.

Rearing these children became the basis for an emerging and growing kids' culture. Scout troops for both boys and girls sprang up. Little League teams were formed. Kids were enrolled in music and dance classes after school.

Far from being encouraged to be "seen and not heard," as in earlier times, Baby Boomers were often at the center of the families' activities in suburban communities. Dr. Benjamin Spock's books about the care of young children were added to nearly every parent's library. Spock thought it was important for parents to treat their children as individuals and respond to situations with flexibility. Believing that happy children turn into well-adjusted adults, Spock encouraged parents to raise their kids with warmth and understanding rather than strict discipline.

The Baby Boom affected many aspects of family life. Because women traditionally had the primary role in child rearing, Spock's books were directed mainly toward mothers. This emphasis helped strengthen traditional ideas about the proper division of labor within the family. Women focused more attention on the home and children; men more often became the sole wage earners.

Many women accepted their role. At the same time, being a homemaker was not entirely satisfying for some women. During the war, when so many young men were stationed overseas, women had often shown that they could work in factories and offices. Now these same women were being told that they should be content to stay at home and raise children and do domestic chores instead of working outside the home for pay. This was fine for some, but not for all.

Betty Friedan's *The Feminine Mystique,* published in 1962, addressed these women's dissatisfactions. This book raised many questions—some of them uncomfortable—about the kinds of lives these suburban homemakers were leading. Friedan asked how educated women could be satisfied with a life of diapers, car pools, and peanut butter sandwiches. She put into words the uneasy feelings of many homemakers and paved the way for the women's movement of the 1960s.

Some women, though, did not have the choice of whether to go to work. To buy a home of their own and move to an area with good schools for the kids, some families needed two wage earners. Women

in these families had to work. Still other women who had worked during the war were squeezed out of their jobs by returning veterans and were forced to work at other jobs for lower wages. Working women were usually limited to certain kinds of jobs, such as teaching and clerical office work, that lacked many chances for promotion. The gap between men's and women's salaries grew.

City Limits

While many Americans moved into the suburbs, changes were also taking place in the cities. Increased factory production during the war and the booming 1950s hastened the migration of blacks from the rural South to both northern and southern cities to find jobs. Many Puerto Ricans and Native Americans also came to the cities of the East and Midwest during this time to escape rural poverty. And as more minority groups were moving into urban areas, more and more whites moved to the suburbs. Many whites left the cities to distance themselves from the conditions of the poor or because of their own racial **prejudice.**

In many suburban areas minorities were purposely excluded. It was difficult, if not impossible, for black and Hispanic families to move into all-white suburbs. Bankers and real estate agents helped white suburban residents enforce their racial prejudices by denying loans to or harassing minority buyers. Even well-to-do, respected members of the black community, like baseball player Willie Mays and actor Sidney Poitier, were unable to find housing in

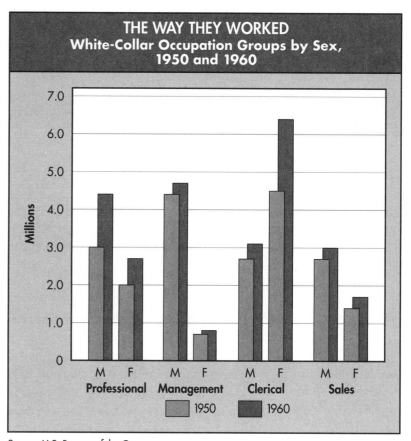

THE WAY THEY WORKED
White-Collar Occupation Groups by Sex, 1950 and 1960

Source: U.S. Bureau of the Census.

wealthy white communities. Yet not all the suburbs were white. Some mainly black suburbs sprang up on the edges of the cities, providing some mobility to a growing black middle class. But by and large, **de facto segregation** divided the cities from the suburbs in both the North and the South.

Migration was changing city neighborhoods as well. Though some minority residents found the economic success they had sought in the city, a great many did not. Most faced **discrimination**, and many were either underpaid or unemployed. All-black or all-Hispanic areas of cities, called **ghettos,** became increasingly crowded. Conditions worsened as older housing structures decayed. Aided by federal housing grants, many cities

▲ During the 1950s the white-collar workforce grew in every sector. The number of women in these occupations grew nearly twice as fast as the number of men. More than half of these women had clerical jobs; males dominated every other sector.

▲ A group of Mexicans awaits transportation to a New Mexico cotton ranch in 1948. During World War II and after, the American government gave seasonal work permits to Mexican *braceros* (temporary workers) for farm labor. Mexicans and Mexican-Americans made up the largest group of migrant farm workers in the United States. Following the changing harvest of crops from state to state, these workers did backbreaking labor for low pay and with terrible living conditions.

began "urban renewal" programs. Their stated goals were to modernize housing and improve the quality of life in cities. Yet these urban renewal programs often resulted in the demolition of lower-income neighborhoods in favor of office buildings or high-rent apartments. The residents of these areas were forced to move elsewhere, sometimes into newly built public housing projects, sometimes into slums.

As many of the poorest Americans were thus hidden from view within the inner city, it became widely believed among the middle class in the 1950s that poverty in America no longer existed. This myth was exploded with the publication in 1962 of Michael Harrington's *The Other America,* which called attention to the millions of people living in poverty in cities and in places like rural Appalachia. For the majority of Americans not left behind by prosperity, however, the reality was a rising standard of living and an improving way of life.

POLITICS AFTER THE NEW DEAL

In President Harry S. Truman's first address to a joint session of Congress on April 16, 1945, he said that he would not relax the efforts made under Franklin Roosevelt's New Deal "to improve the lot of the common people." But taking the country from war to peace was a huge task for the untested president.

Under the New Deal, the role of the federal government had grown—along with its size. While Democrats and liberals supported the New Deal and its reforms, conservative Republicans were wary of this new, bigger role for American government. Once the war was over and the economy seemed to be back on its feet, many conservatives hoped that the regulation of industry would be cut back. Truman and other Democrats pushed to continue the reform agenda.

Which Path to Follow?

One test of the government's role after World War II came over **inflation,** or rising prices. Business leaders wanted the government to lift wartime price controls and return to a mostly free-market economy, in which the laws of supply and demand dictate prices. Workers wanted a bigger share of rising profits. Inflation, stimulated by a huge demand for consumer goods, worsened as prices and wages mounted to keep up with each other. Truman eventually removed the price controls and tried to persuade businesses to keep their prices down voluntarily. Prices soared nevertheless through 1946.

The president was also tested by labor strikes. During the war, workers had earned good wages, while government-controlled prices remained low. The sharp inflation of 1946 was a real threat to their new prosperity. The period following the war was marked by demands for higher wages and by many strikes. Labor unions grew stronger. Concerned that some strikes were holding up production of consumer goods, Truman took some unusual steps to stop them. During a 1946 railroad strike, he went before Congress to propose drafting rail workers into the military so he could then order them to work. While Truman was making his speech, the strike was settled, but labor leaders were angered by the proposal.

While the president was taking emergency steps, Republicans in Congress pressed to limit the power of labor unions, whom they blamed for inflation. To curb union activities, they drafted the Taft-Hartley Act, which became law over Truman's veto (see Business and Economy). A victory for conservatives, the bill was made possible by large Republican gains in the 1946 elections. These gains reflected a renewed conservative strength in American politics.

The size and influence of the federal government continued to grow, however, and many new measures had the support of both political parties. The success of the GI Bill of 1944 had set a new pattern for the government's role in supporting unemployed workers. The Employment Act of 1946 went even further to bring about a permanent shift in policy toward the economy and employment. The president and Congress now had leading roles in keeping unemployment low and watching over the free-market economy (see Business and Economy).

America and its government had arrived at a crossroads, which was symbolized by Truman's domestic struggles. Truman hoped to extend the New Deal with a program he called the "Fair Deal." The Fair Deal included plans for national health insurance, aid to education, public housing, and farm price supports. Truman faced strong opposition from conservatives in Congress, led by Senator Robert A. Taft, who wished to see less New Deal and not more. Nicknamed "Mr. Republican," Taft and his allies held up Truman's Fair Deal, and they felt confident the American people would back them up in the upcoming presidential election.

Truman Wins Again

After a 14-state tour, Republican representative Everett Dirksen of Illinois wired presidential candidate Thomas E. Dewey on election eve: "Your victory is assured and will be bigger than you think. You have a date with destiny." On the morning of November 4, 1948, the real victor—President Harry S. Truman—laughed as he held up the *Chicago Tribune* headline: DEWEY DEFEATS TRUMAN. Truman then said, "I do not feel elated at the victory. I feel overwhelmed with responsibility."

The campaign had been tough. The strong civil rights plank on the Democratic platform led southern

► On the day after his close victory, Truman beams as he holds an early edition of the *Chicago Tribune*. The paper had wrongly proclaimed his defeat based on early returns.

conservative "Dixiecrats" to form a third party, placing South Carolina senator Strom Thurmond on their own ticket. Dewey had run strongly against Roosevelt in 1944, and he expected to defeat Truman easily. Truman's surprise victory was due partly to the support of minorities and organized labor, which came back to Truman after his veto of the Taft-Hartley Act. His exhausting "whistle-stop" campaign across the nation by train also won votes. Finally, as Democrats made gains in Congress as well, voters endorsed the president's party and the New Deal tradition.

Truman's second term did not go smoothly. Republicans and Democrats voting together largely doomed the Fair Deal. Some embarrassing scandals in his administration undermined Truman's popularity. Foreign policy problems in China and Korea made people question his leadership.

The communist scare aroused general concern. He decided not to run again in 1952.

Truman did score some successes in implementing his Fair Deal programs. The Social Security system was broadened, the minimum wage was increased, and low-income housing **subsidies** were begun by the 1949 Housing Act. Finally, President Truman was able to use his executive power to promote a more liberal policy on race. He ordered the integration of the armed forces. He also took action to achieve fairer employment practices in federal agencies and defense industries.

America Likes Ike

Buttons proclaiming "I Like Ike" were a familiar sight during the campaign of 1952. Dwight D. Eisenhower, the popular general who had led the World War II victory in Europe, accepted the Republican nomination. GOP leaders believed correctly that his personal appeal would ensure his success at the polls. His selection of Richard M. Nixon of California as his running mate was politically wise. Nixon was perceived as young, shrewd, conservative, and anticommunist. He also represented the political interests of the increasingly important western states. Midway through the campaign, though, Nixon was nearly dropped from the ticket because of reports that he had accepted improper campaign contributions. In a nationwide television address, Nixon defended his action, stating that the only gift he had kept was a cocker spaniel named Checkers.

Republicans responded favorably to the "Checkers" speech, and Ike kept him on the ticket. The Eisenhower-Nixon team swept the election by 6 million votes over a Democratic ticket headed by Adlai E. Stevenson, the liberal governor of Illinois. A country moving increasingly toward the suburbs and the South and West had chosen a leader whose "middle-of-the-road" views mirrored their own.

As politician and president, Eisenhower was guided by neither conservative nor liberal ideals; rather, he led the country on a course of cautious change. In private he opposed the idea of too much government control, but in the long run, his administration actually expanded the federal role.

Eisenhower took a businesslike approach with a military style of management. He delegated authority freely and employed "consensus decision making," or input from a variety of people, to make policy.

Big business was well represented in his cabinet and regulatory agencies. His domestic policy encouraged private enterprise, turning over atomic energy development to private companies. In spite of a recession in 1957 and 1958, the economy continued to thrive. He also left office in 1961 with the largest deficit up to that time.

Eisenhower did not push for any progressive social legislation, and his administration took little initiative to enforce the important civil rights reforms of his era. Despite Eisenhower's views, however, federal spending on social programs continued to grow, in the form of aid to education, housing programs, and increases to Social Security and the minimum wage. In 1957 the interstate highway system was begun. And the National Aeronautics and Space Administration (NASA) was created in 1958 to compete in the new "space race" with Russia.

Eisenhower's later years in office were marked by health problems, foreign policy crises, and detachment. But throughout his two terms, Ike remained popular, and he kept the country on a steady course. His presidency has come to symbolize the era he governed.

THE CHILL IN U.S.-SOVIET RELATIONS

As World War II ended, the United States hoped most of all to lead the world into a new era of democracy, economic expansion, and free

ALASKA AND HAWAII GAIN STATEHOOD

On June 30, 1958, Congress approved Alaskan statehood. President Eisenhower formally declared Alaska the forty-ninth state in the Union on January 3, 1959. On August 21, 1959, Hawaii was admitted to the Union, making it the fiftieth state.

Alaska became by far the largest state in land area, being more than twice the size of Texas. At the same time, it had until the 1980s the smallest population in the Union. It now ranks forty-ninth, ahead of Wyoming only.

Hawaii had been vying for statehood since 1903, but the request was not seriously considered until the late 1930s. Then the question of Hawaii's statehood was put off again until 1945. Fourteen years later, after much debate, Hawaii achieved its goal. It was the first state whose majority was of Asian descent.

trade. But unresolved disagreements between the Soviets and the Americans at the Yalta and Potsdam conferences at war's end caused their shaky alliance to fall apart. The U.S. government believed strongly that the people of Eastern Europe themselves should determine the kind of government they wanted. The Soviets, whose land and economy were devastated by World War II, wanted to regain a sphere of political and economic influence. Differences between the two sides were aggravated by the Soviet fear that the capitalist governments would eventually try to destroy communism, and by the U.S. belief that the Soviets wanted to dominate the world.

As the Soviets began to use military force to install communist governments in Eastern Europe, Americans worried that they might try to dominate Western Europe as well. Fears of Soviet expansion caused American policymakers to take a more active role in containing communism. The competition for the control of Germany and other areas became known as the Cold War, a tense battle of politics rather than a shooting war.

A New Threat

The U.S. government now had to split its attention between the activities of the Soviet Union and getting America itself back to normal. The Soviets were putting pressure on Turkey and Greece to give them control of key waterways. To counteract that threat, Truman declared in 1947 that the United States would give economic and military aid to those countries. The policy of giving support to coun-

tries threatened by communism—known as the "Truman Doctrine"—became a cornerstone of American foreign policy in the Cold War.

The United States was especially concerned with rebuilding and maintaining stability in Western Europe. A massive aid program called the "Marshall Plan" was started in 1947. Over the next five years, it gave more than $12 billion to 17 European countries to rescue their war-torn economies. In April 1949 representatives from 12 noncommunist nations gathered in Washington, D.C., to sign into being the North Atlantic Treaty Organization (NATO), to counter Soviet aggression in Europe. This was the first time that the United States had taken part in a peacetime military alliance with other nations.

The Truman Doctrine, the Marshall Plan, and NATO all reflected the Truman administration's growing concern with the Soviet Union. Its policy was also influenced by the idea of **containment.** This strategy was developed by George Kennan, advisor to Secretary of State Dean Acheson. In an article for the journal *Foreign Affairs,* Kennan (writing in public as "Mr. X") recommended preventing Soviet expansion by challenging the spread of communism at different places around the world.

Disagreements between the Soviets and the United States about how Korea should be governed heated up the Cold War and became a critical test of containment. After some initial disputes, the United Nations established the 38th parallel as an international boundary between communist

Korea: The Undeclared War

▲ General Douglas MacArthur (right) visits the front lines above the town of Suwon, South Korea, in January 1951. North Korean and Chinese troops had taken nearby Seoul a few weeks earlier.

The land of Korea was divided after World War II between a Soviet-occupied zone, the North, and an American-occupied zone, the South. Struggle for control over all of Korea continued even after the United Nations formally divided the country at the 38th parallel. The Republic of Korea, depending on agriculture and U.S. aid for economic survival, was established in the South under Syngman Rhee. Kim Il Sung ruled the mainly industrial Democratic People's Republic in the North.

On the morning of June 25, 1950, North Korean guns opened fire on South Korean troops at the border. Soon tens of thousands of troops crossed the 38th parallel. The main attack followed, with North Korean tanks advancing toward Seoul, the South Korean capital.

The United States requested an emergency session of the U.N. Security Council, which called for an end to the assault. When the North Koreans did not obey, the Security Council asked that "the members of the United Nations furnish such assistance to the Republic of Korea as may be necessary to repel the armed attack and to restore international peace and security in the area."

President Truman and Secretary of State Dean Acheson concluded that the Soviet Union was directing North Korea's assault. Without obtaining a formal congressional declaration of war, Truman moved naval vessels into the Formosa Strait. On June 30, the joint chiefs of staff ordered General Douglas MacArthur to deploy naval, air, and ground forces. The U.N. made MacArthur commander of the combined forces. Seventeen nations sent troops, and many others sent supplies or medical units. This "police action" was the first time a world body had acted militarily to stop aggression.

In a bold move, MacArthur's troops landed at Inchon and cut North Korean supply lines. By the first of October, 1950, they had pushed the North Koreans out of the South. On October 19, the North Korean capital, Pyongyang, fell. U.N. forces pushed north to the Yalu River. Victory seemed at hand.

The push toward Manchuria drew the Chinese into the war, however, and U.N. troops were forced into a long retreat. At this point, the U.N. just wanted to contain communist forces along the 38th parallel while negotiating the war's end. But MacArthur wanted to fight an "entirely new war"—against Red China—which ran against Truman's wishes. Truman fired MacArthur, but the general still received a hero's welcome at home.

After two more years of stalemate, the two sides agreed to a truce. Millions of Koreans had been killed or left homeless, and several thousand Americans were killed. Nevertheless, the American public generally supported this undeclared war.

North Korea and noncommunist South Korea. Tension between the two sides climaxed on June 25, 1950, when thousands of North Korean troops poured over the border. Without obtaining a formal declaration of war from Congress, Truman sent General Douglas MacArthur with U.S. forces to fight the North Koreans.

Entering the Atomic Age

While the Korean War flared, a whole new stage of the Cold War was coming into being. The atom bombs that were dropped on Hiroshima on August 6, 1945, and on Nagasaki three days later had changed forever the destructive force of warfare and the balance of power in the world. At that time, the United States was the only nation with atomic weapons. But in 1949, to the surprise of the American government and the shock of the American people, the Soviet Union successfully tested its own atom bomb.

The A-bomb was just the beginning. After the Soviet Union set off its A-bomb, the United States began developing a larger "super bomb," the hydrogen bomb. A group of scientists, led by J. Robert Oppenheimer, advised against developing this devastating weapon, but the military and the Atomic Energy Commission supported the idea to preserve America's nuclear dominance. The first successful H-bomb test was conducted in the Pacific Ocean on November 1, 1952.

Nuclear tests became regular occurrences in the 1950s. At the time, most people, including many scientists, were unaware of the long-term effects of exploding nuclear weapons. A 1954 H-bomb test at Bikini Atoll first brought attention to the dangers of **fallout**. Radioactive ash fell on a wide area of the Pacific Ocean, and some fishermen nearly a hundred miles from the blast became sick from the radiation. A movement began to ban nuclear explosions in the atmosphere, which led in time to the 1963 Partial Test Ban Treaty.

Atomic weapons and the threat of nuclear war had a profound impact on American society. In an era when the level of comfort was increasing in so many ways, "the bomb" loomed as an imminent danger. It brought fear and uncertainty, especially about how the Russians might use it. That fear increased when the Russians exploded their own H-bomb. The dangers of fallout created new concerns in America and all over the world as people realized that the atomic rivalry of Cold War enemies could alter the whole planet.

The Arms Race

The atomic age brought changes to American foreign policy as well. President Eisenhower and his secretary of state, John Foster Dulles, advocated using the threat of "massive retaliation"—nuclear bombardment—to discourage the Soviets from expanding their influence. Several times during Eisenhower's administration, the United States almost reached the point of military intervention in international crises. Dulles's apparent willingness to go to the brink of war came to be called "brinkmanship." But the threat of massive retaliation ultimately failed to stop

Soviet aggression, most notably during the Soviet invasion of Hungary in 1956 (see The World).

The idea of massive retaliation radically changed defense systems and strategies. The United States spent more and more on nuclear weapons and ways to deliver them. When the Soviets stepped up their nuclear spending, the **arms race** was on. After the Soviet space satellite *Sputnik* was launched, U.S. news stories warned of a "missile gap," or Soviet dominance in the technology of weapons and space. Though a missile gap did not in fact exist, it and *Sputnik* became the grounds for further increases in military spending. The arms race quickened.

Even as the Cold War buildup increased, however, Eisenhower ushered in an era of superpower

meetings and arms-reduction talks. The Korean War ended shortly after Joseph Stalin's death in 1953, and the Cold War seemed to thaw a little. Eisenhower's 1955 **summit** in Geneva, Switzerland, with new Soviet chairman Nikita Khrushchev began a pattern of dialogue between the two countries. Though little was agreed on, the "Spirit of Geneva" became a source of optimism and the basis for future talks.

Eisenhower reached the peak of his popularity both at home and abroad after the Geneva summit. Though "waging peace" became his motto, Cold War crises continued to arise. During Ike's last year in office, an American U-2 plane, captained by Francis Gary Powers, was shot down while on a spy mission over the Soviet Union. The

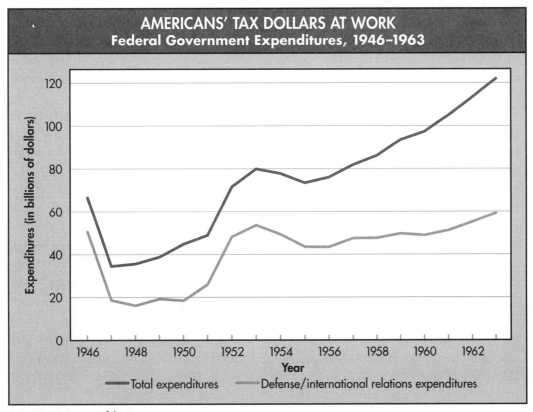

AMERICANS' TAX DOLLARS AT WORK
Federal Government Expenditures, 1946–1963

Total expenditures — Defense/international relations expenditures

Source: U.S. Bureau of the Census.

◄ Defense spending dropped significantly after World War II, but it shot up again during the Korean conflict. The arms race and other Cold War military spending made this heightened level a permanent fixture in the federal budget.

► Pilot Francis Gary Powers holds a model of his U-2 plane as he prepares to testify before Congress in 1962. Shot down on May 1, 1960, over the Soviet Union, Powers spent nearly two years in a Soviet prison. He was exchanged for a Soviet spy jailed in the United States.

RED SCARE LAWS

In the late 1940s polls showed that an ever-larger number of Americans supported outlawing the Communist party in America altogether. Some voices pointed out that banning political activity in peacetime ran counter to the freedoms granted by the Bill of Rights. But as the fear of communism grew, this fact became more and more obscured.

The McCarran Act, passed by Congress in 1950, put strict limits on communist political activity in the United States. While it did not ban the party outright, the act required communists to register with the government. People who were communists could not travel abroad or work in certain jobs.

During this time many states passed laws that required teachers to swear "loyalty oaths" that they were not communists. Some laws made it impossible to teach certain ideas, because teachers could be fired for appearing "disloyal."

incident embarrassed American officials and led the enraged Soviets to halt an upcoming summit. Meanwhile, Fidel Castro, the leader of the Cuban revolution, openly allied his country with the Soviet Union. And the unresolved status of Germany remained a source of Cold War tension.

In spite of these roller-coaster events, however, Eisenhower kept the United States out of any major military conflicts during his administration. The United States continued to intervene throughout the world and military budgets remained high, but the unthinkable nuclear war was avoided. As he left office, the president expressed concern about what he called the "military-industrial complex"—the Defense Department and leading defense contractors—which he feared was becoming too powerful. Despite this warning, Cold War military spending continued to grow under his successors.

COLD WAR IN AMERICA

On February 9, 1950, Wisconsin's Senator Joseph McCarthy spoke to a Republican women's club in Wheeling, West Virginia. His topic was the spread of communism, from the USSR to Eastern Europe and then to China. He told the group that communists in the government were trying to undermine U.S. foreign policy. He waved a piece of paper and declared: "I have here in my hand a list of 205 State Department employees who were members of the Communist Party."

In the weeks that followed, two things became clear about McCarthy's list. The first was that its existence was doubtful—he did not show it to anyone, and indeed the numbers he gave reporters kept changing. A Senate committee formed to investigate his charges quickly dismissed them as untrue.

But the second thing to become clear was that no matter how shaky McCarthy's claims were, they gave his career an enormous boost. In an era of fear and Cold War tensions, anticommunism was good politics.

From Spy Fears to a Red Hunt

In postwar America two famous spy cases became the focus of public speculation, concern, and controversy. In 1948 the House Un-American Activities Committee (HUAC) began investigating mysterious charges that Alger Hiss, a former government official under Roosevelt, had passed secret documents to the USSR. Hiss's accuser was Whittaker Chambers, a former *Time* magazine editor, who told the committee that both he and Hiss had been communists in the 1930s. Hiss denied everything, and throughout the case it was difficult for the public to tell which man was telling the truth. Though Hiss was eventually jailed for perjury and his reputation was tarnished, the public remained divided.

Formed in the 1930s to investigate communism in America, HUAC was not well known until communism became a hot topic in the late 1940s. The dramatic revelations surrounding the Hiss case brought attention to the committee's anticommunist cause, and especially to Richard M. Nixon, who led the investigation. Nixon, serving his first term in Congress, described the case as a "small part of the whole shocking story of Communist espionage in the United States." Some people began to believe this was true.

Then, in 1950, another astonishing spy case unfolded. When news of the Soviets' A-bomb became known, the government tried to find out how they were able to develop one so quickly. An answer seemed to come from Klaus Fuchs, a scientist who had helped build

The CIA: Cold War Intelligence

The new conditions and policies of the Cold War required modernized government machinery to keep up with them. The National Security Act of 1947 unified the armed services under the Department of Defense and created the National Security Council to advise the president on matters related to intelligence and security. The act also established the Central Intelligence Agency (CIA). Its primary functions were to gather intelligence information outside the United States and to analyze global political situations.

The act gave the CIA broad powers with few details on how to use them. The CIA director reported directly to the president, so the agency could act in secrecy. This gave the White House enormous new power, allowing it to act or react without con-gressional approval. As the Cold War intensified, Congress gave the CIA unlimited funds to carry on secret activities under the direction of the White House.

▼ ▼ ▼

The National Security Act of 1947 gave the CIA broad powers with few details on how to use them.

Given this free rein, the role of the CIA grew. From its early jobs of spying on the Soviets and funding pro-Western groups in Europe, the agency went on to more active secret operations. It helped overthrow the leaders of Iran and Guatemala in 1954, and it propped up pro-Western governments in Laos and Vietnam during the 1950s. These events set a pattern for using the CIA for intervention abroad that has lasted until today.

Margaret Chase Smith: A Plea for Reason

◄ Margaret Chase Smith was first elected to the Senate in 1948 after serving four terms in the House. She followed a generally independent course in Congress, taking a liberal stance on many domestic issues and a conservative one on foreign policy and defense matters. She worked hard to improve the status of women in the military.

On June 1, 1950, the first-term senator from Maine strode up to the Senate podium holding the text of a speech that she had shown to only a few. She had reason to be nervous. It was her first major speech before the Senate, and it was critical of her own Republican party.

As Smith spoke, journalists looked over the Senate floor with full attention. The object of her speech, a quickly rising senator from Wisconsin, was also present.

"Those of us who shout the loudest about Americanism in making character assassinations are all too frequently those who . . . ignore some of the basic principles of Americanism: the right to criticize, the right to hold unpopular beliefs, the right to protest, the right of independent thought," she declared. "The exercise of these rights should not cost one single American citizen his reputation or his right to a livelihood, nor should he be in danger . . . merely because he happens to know someone who holds unpopular beliefs."

Smith and six other Republican senators had drafted a "declaration of conscience," which was critical of Senator Joseph McCarthy and the "witch hunts" that were becoming a part of public life. The proclamation was politically risky, but Smith went on to serve 22 more years in the Senate.

the first nuclear bombs at Los Alamos, New Mexico. Fuchs admitted to passing atomic secrets to the Soviets, and he named several others who had helped. The case became focused on a New York couple, Ethel and Julius Rosenberg.

The Rosenbergs went on trial in 1951. Their case, too, was surrounded by confusing and conflicting testimony. The government's prosecution was controversial, but it won a conviction. The Rosenbergs *had* been members of the Communist party, and this fact was damaging enough in the panicky era. They were sentenced to death as spies.

The Rosenbergs' firm denial of their guilt won them many supporters, and their harsh sentence aroused public outcry around the world. Were they traitors or merely victims of anticommunist hysteria? After failed appeals to the Supreme Court and President Eisenhower, the Rosenbergs died in the electric chair on June 19, 1953. They were the first American civilians to be executed for spying.

The amount of publicity in these cases caused much speculation—usually overblown—by politicians and the media about communists and spies in government posts. President Truman ignited these concerns in 1947 with his massive "loyalty program," a plan to screen all government employees. The program set out to fire "security risks," but its scope went well beyond a search for actual spies. Many people were dismissed on the basis of hearsay evidence, or they were removed for entirely unrelated matters. Pressure was growing to root out communists, and civil liberties were being trampled in the process.

The Rise and Fall of Joe McCarthy

It was this atmosphere that set the stage for Joe McCarthy. The stir aroused by his Wheeling speech led him to continue leaking accusations to an anxious press. McCarthy was becoming a celebrity, and over the next few years he gained considerable power in Washington. He put pressure on government officials to toe his conservative line or risk being labeled a communist or communist "sympathizer." McCarthy ruined careers by smearing reputations. The tactics he used in investigations and hearings—creating unfounded suspicion, using secret informants and leaks, and presuming guilt by association—came to symbolize the era.

His recklessness offended many around him, including other Republicans. But party leaders could not ignore his growing public support, and they welcomed the political points he earned by attacking the Truman administration. But even after Eisenhower took over, the senator continued to exert his influence over the White House. Ike and McCarthy eventually squared off over the U.S. Army.

In early 1954 McCarthy's investigation of the Army led to televised hearings. For 36 days the country tuned in to see McCarthy at work. What they saw was not a crusader, but a man who bullied witnesses and twisted their words. Television damaged McCarthy's public image, and it made a hero of his opponent, the Army's lawyer, Joseph Welch. Welch's words helped break

McCarthy's spell: "Until this moment, Senator, I think I never really gauged your cruelty or your recklessness. . . . Have you left no sense of decency?" McCarthy's quick rise was followed by a quicker fall.

McCarthy did not create the public anxiety over communists, spies, and the bomb, but he used it ruthlessly. The term *McCarthyism* came to define the era when anticommunist hysteria divided the country. But McCarthyism did not begin or end with McCarthy himself. Many other probes—often on slim grounds—were conducted by HUAC and similar committees on the state and local levels. The climate of mistrust spread from government hearing rooms to the nation's businesses, universities, and even to Hollywood (see Arts and Entertainment). The hysteria eased somewhat with the temporary thaw in U.S.-Soviet relations marked by the Geneva summit. But its effects—especially for those who lost their jobs and their reputations—were felt long after.

> "*This is no time for men who oppose Senator McCarthy's methods to keep silent.*"
>
> —Edward R. Murrow, *See It Now*, 1954

▼ Under the glare of television lights, Senator Joseph McCarthy discusses communist organizations in the United States during the Army-McCarthy hearings. Army counsel Joseph Welch is seated to his right. Though Welch looks discouraged after an angry clash with McCarthy, the moment would mark a turning point in the hearings. Viewers at home were applauding the strong scolding he gave the senator.

BLACKS BATTLE FOR EQUALITY

"I am an invisible man. I am invisible, understand, because people refuse to see me," Ralph Ellison wrote in *Invisible Man,* a novel about black life, in 1952. It brought to national attention the betrayal of African-Americans by America's mostly white culture. Ellison predicted that blacks, "in a state of hibernation," would soon take action. He was right.

The modern civil rights movement actually began with World War II. Many blacks went to war to fight for democracy, for the American way of life. Following the Battle of the Bulge, they served in mainly desegregated units. When they came home, they looked for the human rights they had fought for. They found instead the prejudice and racial discrimination they remembered from the past.

Demands for fairer treatment in civilian life gave force to the struggle for racial equality. Black groups and leaders arose to undertake that struggle. CORE, the Congress of Racial Equality, was founded in 1942 to combat racial discrimination, and it grew quickly in the 1950s under the leadership of James Farmer. Membership in the National Association for the Advancement of Colored People (NAACP) increased sevenfold during the war. Adam Clayton Powell became a Democratic congressman from New York City in 1945, representing a growing urban political base.

Segregation on Trial

In 1896 the Supreme Court had ruled in *Plessy v. Ferguson* that the Fourteenth Amendment did not necessarily abolish distinctions based on color. It stated that segregation was allowable as long as facilities were provided for both races. The principle of "separate but equal" became the basis for many states' segregation laws.

Among the laws protected by the *Plessy* decision were those that dictated separate schools for

Major Supreme Court Decisions on Civil Rights, 1946–1963

Morgan v. Virginia	1946	Declared unconstitutional state laws requiring segregated seating on interstate buses on the grounds that such laws had negative impact on interstate commerce.
Sweatt v. Painter	1950	Ruled that state law schools must admit black applicants, even if separate black schools exist. The University of Texas had tried to create a separate law school for a black applicant. The court held that such a school could never equal the quality of the established school.
McLaurin v. Oklahoma State Regents for Higher Education	1950	Stated that once blacks were admitted to a state graduate school, they were free to use all its facilities. The case came about because the University of Oklahoma graduate school had admitted a black student but had assigned him separate tables in classrooms and in the library and cafeteria. The court ruled this separation unequal.
Brown v. Board of Education of Topeka, Kansas	1954	Overturned practice of "separate but equal" public schools for blacks. Signaled the start of U.S. public-school desegregation.
Brown v. Board of Education of Topeka (Brown II)	1955	Set guidelines for ending segregation in public schools. Urged school boards to proceed "with all deliberate speed."
Cooper v. Aaron	1958	Refused a request by Little Rock, Arkansas, school officials for a delay in desegregating their schools.

blacks and whites. While de facto segregation was widespread in the North, most states in the South had laws that enforced segregated schools and colleges. Black activists had long challenged these laws, but as long as states could show that similar facilities were provided for blacks, the courts usually sided with them.

The NAACP and its chief lawyer, Thurgood Marshall, decided that the best way to challenge "separate but equal" would be to show that a truly equal education could not be provided in segregated schools. After a few victories involving graduate schools, the NAACP turned its attention to segregation in public schools.

In 1953 Marshall collected several segregation cases he was trying and brought them all together before the Supreme Court under the name *Brown v. Board of Education of Topeka, Kansas*. He argued that the Court should look again at how "separate but equal" applied to schoolchildren, not only because buildings and supplies were often not equal, but because of the damage to young minds that a segregated system causes. In its landmark 1954 decision, the Court decided unanimously that "separate education facilities are inherently unequal." Separating children by race, it concluded, "generates a feeling of inferiority as to their status in the community that may affect their hearts and minds in a way unlikely ever to be undone."

The Court's decision made school integration the law of the land, but it did not tell states how and when to achieve it. Many school districts, backed by parents and state officials, resisted.

Earl Warren: New Directions for the Court

Many were surprised when President Eisenhower picked Earl Warren as chief justice of the Supreme Court in 1953. Warren was known more as a moderately conservative politician than as a legal scholar. Few could have predicted that he would emerge as a strong defender of civil rights and the architect of decisions that would reshape American society.

Warren took his seat during one of the Court's most important cases. His arrival gave the NAACP the chance to reargue the *Brown* case, but few realized at the time what a break that was. Warren was swayed strongly by their case, and he convinced the other justices to issue a unanimous judgment for change.

▼ ▼ ▼

"*A denial of constitutionally protected rights demands judicial protection; our oath and our office require no less of us.*"

—*Reynolds v. Sims* (1964)

Warren believed that the Supreme Court should rule on the basis of modern interpretations of the Constitution rather than on the basis of past rulings only. To many, this was a radical approach. Yet many of the Warren Court decisions established ideas that are taken for granted today, such as the unlawfulness of segregation. *Baker v. Carr* (1962) reaffirmed the "one person, one vote" principle for equal representation. The decision forced states to maintain balanced voting districts. Warren considered it his most important case.

James Meredith became the first black to attend the University of Mississippi when he enrolled in 1962. His registration was held up by protest riots, during which two people were killed. Meredith succeeded in enrolling, however. He was protected by federal troops until he graduated in 1963.

That same year, Alabama's governor, George Wallace, stood in front of the University of Alabama to prevent blacks from enrolling there. Wallace had been elected in 1962 on a platform of defiant segregation. He eventually yielded to federal pressure and allowed the university to integrate.

The next year the Court issued a ruling that desegregation should be carried out "with all deliberate speed." Officials continued to stall, however. By the start of Eisenhower's second term in 1957, not one child in the Deep South yet attended a desegregated public school.

Central High School in Little Rock, Arkansas, soon became the focus of national attention when the Supreme Court ordered the city to desegregate its public schools for the 1957–1958 school year. The state's governor sidestepped several orders to enforce integration, using the National Guard to turn away black students. Eventually, Eisenhower took federal control of the Guard troops, and they protected the students entering the integrated school. News of ugly words and ac-

tions by white parents and officials raced around the world and dealt a blow to American prestige abroad.

Battling Inequality

Because of *Plessy v. Ferguson*, segregation laws (also called "Jim Crow" laws) existed in most of the South, dictating separate facilities for blacks and whites. Restaurants, schools, buses, hospitals—even cemeteries—were segregated. **Poll taxes** and literacy tests kept many black people from voting. The *Brown* decision brought hope, but the government was taking little action to end discrimination in other areas. It now fell on ordinary people to lead the way for change.

Rosa Parks became a heroine of the civil rights movement in 1955. Tired from a long day at work, she sat down in the front part of a Montgomery, Alabama, bus and

▶ Federal troops escort nine black students to classes at Central High in Little Rock on September 25, 1957. Governor Orval Faubus had delayed their entrance more than three weeks, claiming that he could not ensure their safety. Faubus's actions turned a tense situation into a serious crisis, but integration proceeded nonetheless.

refused to move to the back, where the blacks were supposed to sit. Parks's arrest triggered a bus boycott by the city's black community, organized by the Reverend Martin Luther King Jr. Although its leaders were arrested, the boycott successfully put enormous pressure on the city's white leaders. Blacks used black cab companies and car pools. They walked to work. Black church buses helped out. A year later, the Supreme Court declared Alabama's segregation laws **unconstitutional,** and one struggle for black dignity had been won.

Realizing that people acting individually could have only a limited impact, blacks formed a solid front. The Southern Christian Leadership Conference was formed under King in the late 1950s, and CORE grew. In 1960 the Student Nonviolent Coordinating Committee was formed. These groups shared successful methods of protest, such as the widely publicized **sit-ins** that challenged segregated lunch counters and other facilities. Groups of students would sit at whites-only counters—for days if necessary—until businesses were pressured to change their policies.

In the early 1960s CORE organized a racially mixed group, called "Freedom Riders," to ride interstate buses throughout the South. In 1946 the Supreme Court had outlawed segregation on these buses and in their terminals and restaurants, but no authority had enforced that ruling. The Freedom Riders ultimately succeeded in forcing the hand of the federal government to carry out the Constitution's pledge.

▲ Southern segregation laws dictated separate drinking fountains for blacks and whites.

Civil rights workers, both black and white, faced grave personal dangers. Southern police cars often led Ku Klux Klan raids on black neighborhoods. Police dogs and fire hoses were often turned on marchers, and some activists were beaten or killed. Television pictures of police brutality aroused sympathy for the civil rights cause across the nation.

Political Impact

Civil rights actions sparked legislation to further the cause of equal opportunity. Taking the lead from the Supreme Court, liberal legislators pushed for civil rights laws, but they faced opposition on many fronts. Southern Democrats consistently voted for segregation, and both Republican and Democratic candidates needed their support. President Eisenhower himself never came out strongly in favor of civil rights reforms.

The Civil Rights Act, the first major civil rights bill since Reconstruction, was signed into law in

THE 23RD AMENDMENT
On March 29, 1961, Congress passed the Twenty-third Amendment to the Constitution, giving the citizens of the District of Columbia the right to vote for the president and vice president.

1957. Although compromises were written into it to satisfy the South, it remained an important piece of legislation. It established a commission to investigate denials of civil rights and voting rights. It also gave added responsibility to the attorney general to enforce equal protection under the law. A second bill in 1960 strengthened the measure.

In spite of new laws, civil rights enforcement continued to be lukewarm through most of John F. Kennedy's administration. As a candidate, Kennedy had wavered on civil rights issues, though he did gain Martin Luther King's support. As president, he was reluctant to take an active role in the voter registration movement in the South. In 1963, however, he did take a stronger stand against police brutality during King's civil rights demonstration in Birmingham, Alabama. He also enforced the admission of blacks to the University of Alabama.

Just the Beginning

King organized a massive march on Washington on August 28, 1963, to dramatize the need for more legislation. In front of the Lincoln Memorial he delivered his emotional "I Have a Dream" speech, in which he declared that the movement for equality will not be satisfied "until justice rolls down like waters and righteousness like a mighty stream." *Time* magazine chose King as Man of the Year in January 1964, the first time an African-American had been hon-

Dr. Martin Luther King Jr.: A Man with a Dream

A 27-year-old preacher walked solemnly to his pulpit at the Dexter Avenue Baptist Church in Montgomery, Alabama. "He who passively accepts evil is as much involved in it as he who helps to perpetuate it," he told his congregation. "In order to be true to one's conscience and true to God, a righteous man has no alternative but to refuse to cooperate."

Dr. Martin Luther King Jr. was the son of a Baptist minister and grew up in a middle-class home in Atlanta. He decided to follow his father into the ministry— a vocation well suited to this thoughtful man with an outstanding flair for public speaking.

▼ ▼ ▼

"I have a dream that one day on the red hills of Georgia the sons of former slaves and the sons of former slaveowners will be able to sit down together at the table of brotherhood."

—March on Washington Address (1963)

King's speech was following the teachings of Mahatma Gandhi, India's great political and spiritual leader. King, like Gandhi, preached civil disobedience, or nonviolent resistance to laws. King and other ministers used civil disobedience successfully during the Montgomery bus boycott.

The boycott thrust King into a leading role in the civil rights movement. Its success prompted him and others to continue using nonviolent resistance to press for equality. King faced many dangers with his followers, never asking them to do anything he would not do himself. He was jailed several times, and his life was threatened often. King continued his peaceful fight until April 3, 1968, when, like Gandhi, he was killed by an assassin's bullet.

ored in this way. Later that year he won the Nobel Peace Prize.

In 1964 President Lyndon Johnson pushed a major civil rights bill through Congress over Dixiecrat opposition. But, impatient at the slow progress of nonviolent resistance, some blacks became angry and frustrated, and they looked elsewhere for solutions. Black nationalist movements gained strength. Malcolm X became a spokesperson for Black Muslims, founding the Organization for Afro-American Unity.

Although the civil rights movement succeeded in forcing the passage of key legislation, the struggle for equal opportunity was by no means over. Authorities were still slow to enforce civil rights laws. The prejudices of many whites toward blacks were unchanged. Though blacks regained many political rights, the challenges of economic equality still lay before the nation.

THE PROMISE OF A NEW FRONTIER

The year 1960 saw many American setbacks. Communists had gained a foothold in Cuba, and U.S. influence was declining elsewhere in Latin America. A U-2 spy plane crashed over the Soviet Union on the eve of a summit meeting. The embarrassment of *Sputnik* was still fresh in people's minds. The USSR appeared to be surpassing the United States in arms and space, and who knew in how many other

ways. All this contributed to a national mood of uncertainty and discouragement.

In 1960 Americans elected a young and well-spoken new leader, one who promised to change the direction the country was going in. John Fitzgerald Kennedy had run successfully as a Democrat for a seat in the U.S. House of Representatives in 1946. In 1952, at the age of 35, he defeated Republican Henry Cabot Lodge for the U.S. Senate, even though Lodge was backed by the popular President Eisenhower. The upset was an early indication of Kennedy's appeal to voters.

At the Helm

The election of 1960 was very close. Kennedy put together a highly organized, well-financed campaign with Senator Lyndon Johnson of Texas as his running mate. His Republican opponent, Richard M. Nixon, was the current vice president. Kennedy faced an uphill battle due to his religious background—a Roman Catholic had never been elected president. But he overcame this concern, focusing his campaign on a "New Frontier" for America.

A major turning point of the campaign was a series of debates between the candidates, the first ever to be televised. Kennedy's style turned out to be well suited to TV, and he scored many points with voters because he looked better than Nixon. As president, Kennedy continued to use TV very effectively to inspire confidence in his administration.

On a cold January day in 1961, Kennedy presented his eloquent

▲ President Kennedy delivers his inaugural address. At the right sits the new vice president, Lyndon Johnson.

"*Let every nation know, whether it wishes us well or ill, that we shall pay any price, bear any burden, meet any hardship, support any friend, oppose any foe to assure the survival and the success of liberty.*"

—John F. Kennedy, inaugural address, January 20, 1961

inaugural address. The moment symbolized to many that, as he said, "the torch has been passed to a new generation of Americans." He told a hopeful nation, "Ask not what your country can do for you—ask what you can do for your country."

Once in office, Kennedy tried to turn his broad New Frontier vision of progress into a legislative plan. He recruited "the best and the brightest" from institutions around the country to serve in his administration. But he had trouble pushing programs through Congress. He seemed unwilling to put the weight of his position and public appeal behind them. Many

of his domestic proposals, such as aid to education, civil rights legislation, and Medicare, were stalled until his successor, Lyndon Johnson, got them passed.

The New Frontier's major successes reflect its sense of a renewed national purpose. The Peace Corps and the Alliance for Progress, an aid program for Latin America, helped shape and reaffirm America's leadership role in the world. His commitment to put an American on the moon by the end of the decade became a rallying point for the country.

Focus on the Cold War

The Cold War dominated Kennedy's foreign policy. The defense budget soared. The level of ground forces increased, and nuclear arms were stockpiled. At the same time, however, superpower summit meetings continued. The United States, Great Britain, and the Soviet Union signed a nuclear test ban treaty, and a hotline was set up between the United States and the USSR to communicate during nuclear crises.

Several Cold War crises tested Kennedy's leadership. During the Eisenhower administration, the CIA had devised an invasion of Cuba intended to overthrow Fidel Castro. Though it was badly designed, Kennedy gave approval to the Bay of Pigs invasion, which took place in April 1961. The scheme was a disaster, and Kennedy publicly took the blame for its embarrassing failure.

Kennedy and Soviet premier Khrushchev then faced off over Berlin. Surrounded by East Germany, West Berlin was a haven for people fleeing from the communist East. Khrushchev tried to drive the Western powers out, but Kennedy responded firmly with an increased military presence. East Germany began building its famous wall around West Berlin, and the Berlin crisis eased.

In 1962 the two superpowers clashed in Cuba. The United States discovered that the Soviets were building missile sites there. Kennedy set up a naval and air blockade of weapons shipments to Cuba. The world watched Washington and Moscow for several tense October days while the two superpowers seemed close to war. The crisis ended after the Soviets agreed to tear down the bases and Kennedy promised that the United States would not invade Cuba.

A Hero Falls

In November 1963 Kennedy traveled to Texas to patch up differences between Democratic factions there. While riding in a motorcade through Dallas, he was gunned down by assassin Lee Harvey Oswald and died within an hour. The country was stunned and grief stricken. Many Americans still recall where they were at the moment they heard the news.

Kennedy had become one of American history's most charismatic presidents. His mystique—his Harvard education, youth, charm, and attractive family—became magnified by his death. In reality his administration did not take many bold stands on controversial issues. Yet he came to symbolize both hope for the future and promise unfulfilled. His killing seemed to put a violent end to the comfortable postwar era of prosperity and peace. A period of confusion and conflict was to follow.

◄ Surrounded by the Kennedy family, John Kennedy Jr. touchingly salutes his father's casket as it leaves Washington Cathedral. It was John Jr.'s third birthday.

THE WORLD

The years following World War II were a time of great change. The end of the war signaled the end of European dominance in the world. Rising in its place were the United States, which emerged from the war stronger than it had gone in, and the Soviet Union, which was trying to recover from huge losses. A competition between these two nations soon arose as they pursued their separate goals, each distrusting the motivations of the other. Their rivalry—the Cold War—ushered in a new era of instability and fear, one made more uncertain by a new weapon—the atomic bomb.

The first arena of confrontation was Europe, where the Americans and Russians had fought together during World War II. On the front line lay Germany, defeated in war and divided by the Cold War. The Berlin Wall (above), built by

AT A GLANCE

▶ The Cold War Begins

▶ The New Face of China

▶ European Economic Recovery

▶ Independence Now

▶ The Other Americas

East Germany to halt the flow of its citizens to the West, was one result of the ongoing tension. Hastily erected in 1961, the wall gave real form—in concrete and barbed wire—to the symbolic "Iron Curtain" that separated East from West.

World War II had in one way or another touched every corner of the globe. In its aftermath, governments around the world were undergoing change. Many became the focus of power struggles between the superpowers. Countries in Africa, Latin America, Asia, and the Middle East received global attention as they struggled to gain independence and enter the modern industrialized world. These Third World nations, although still dependent on the major powers for support, had a new voice in the world community—the United Nations.

DATAFILE

World population	1950	1960
Total	2.5 bil.	3 bil.
Africa	224 mil.	281 mil.
Asia	1.4 bil.	1.7 bil.
Australia and Oceania	12 mil.	15 mil.
Central and South America	165 mil.	218 mil.
Europe	393 mil.	425 mil.
North America	166 mil.	199 mil.
USSR	180 mil.	214 mil.

OUT OF WORK
Unemployment in Selected Countries, 1950 and 1960

Source: European History Statistics.

THE COLD WAR BEGINS

People danced in the streets the world over, from Moscow to Manhattan, on August 14, 1945, the day Japan surrendered and the **Allies** claimed final victory over the **Axis** countries. As the celebrations faded, however, the immediate future for people in Europe, Asia, and Africa was uncertain. This second world war had been won by powerful countries fighting together, and this joint effort signaled some hope for the world's future. Not many people could have foreseen how quickly the partnership between the Soviet Union and the United States would dissolve. Within a few years, the two would enter an era of intense competition, the Cold War.

A Common Enemy Creates an Uneasy Alliance

Great Britain, the United States, and the Soviet Union became allies because they shared one goal—to put an end to **fascism,** in the form of the aggressive dictatorships of Germany, Italy, and Japan. Apart from a common enemy, the communist Soviet Union and the two Western democracies had very little else in common.

Underlying their differences were their opposing forms of government and economy. The Soviet political system was a dictatorship controlled by the Communist party; the Western countries were representative democracies. The Soviet economy was based in theory on collective ownership and was tightly restricted by the state; the regulated market economies of

After the war, an important issue confronting the victorious Allies was the treatment of German Nazi leaders. The United States, Great Britain, France, and the USSR agreed to establish an International Military Tribunal (court) to try Nazi political and military leaders as war criminals. The trials were held at the German city of Nuremberg, the site of many Nazi rallies.

In 1945 and 1946, 19 Nazis were convicted of war crimes or "crimes against humanity." Of these, 12 were sentenced to death, including Hitler's second-in-command, Hermann Göring.

The Nuremberg trials sparked some controversy over the legal issues involved. Critics questioned whether crimes committed during war should be held against individuals, because their acts were sanctioned by their own government.

the West were based on the principles of **capitalism**—the private ownership and operation of the means of production. Communist leaders criticized the capitalist system for taking advantage of the working class and creating inequalities of wealth. In turn, the Western countries were distrustful of Soviet communism and its lack of freedoms.

The Western countries were especially mistrustful of Joseph Stalin, the powerful and unpredictable Soviet leader. In 1939, Stalin had made a secret agreement with Germany's Adolf Hitler. They both invaded Poland and split the country between them. The next year, the Soviets moved into Latvia, Lithuania, and Estonia. Although the Allies took the side of the Soviets when Germany attacked the USSR in 1941, they kept in mind how Stalin had tried to play on both sides of the fence.

From the beginning, the alliance was strained by disagreements over how the war should be fought. The Soviet Union was under heavy German attack. Stalin became anxious for the Allies to attack Germany from the west—through France—to relieve the pressure on the Russian front. But the Allies concentrated their efforts first in Africa and then in Italy, fearing the heavy losses they would likely incur in an invasion of France. They did not invade from the west until June 6, 1944. During the three years preceding, many millions of Russians died and thousands of villages were destroyed by the Germans. The delay of the second front became a sore point for the Soviets.

A spirit of agreement concealed these tensions when the three allies met in the Soviet city of Yalta a few months before the end of the war. The "Big Three" leaders—Stalin, Great Britain's Winston Churchill, and an ailing Franklin D. Roosevelt—came together to discuss what would happen to Germany and the territory it held when the war ended.

Each man came to the meeting with definite goals. Churchill and Stalin were concerned about the future security of their own nations. They wanted to prevent Germany from rising again. Stalin looked to protect his country by gaining more control over Eastern Europe. Churchill wanted to revive France and protect Britain's interests in Europe. Roosevelt called for free elections and free trade.

The Soviet Union, hit hardest by the war, wanted a defeated Germany to pay more than $20 billion in damages. The United States and Great Britain wanted to treat Germany in a way that would not repeat the conditions that led to Hitler's rise to power. They did not want to squeeze the life out of Germany but to rebuild it, preferably in their own image.

Finally, the Big Three agreed to disagree. They decided to split the defeated country into occupation zones. Germany was divided into four sections, one each governed by the United States, Great Britain, France, and the USSR. The German capital, Berlin, which lay within the Soviet zone, was also divided into four parts. It was agreed that elections would be held in Germany, Poland, and other occupied countries in the future.

From Allies to Enemies

Yalta was the high point of the Big Three alliance. After Roosevelt died, a rather undiplomatic Harry S. Truman took charge. He met with Stalin and Churchill (who would be replaced during the meeting by a new prime minister, Clement Attlee) at Potsdam, Germany, after the German surrender, to make more plans for postwar Europe. Truman took a hard line with the Soviet leader. He had just learned about the development of the atomic bomb, so he had a strong bargaining position. Churchill later said that Truman "told the Russians where they got off and generally bossed the whole meeting." More agreements were made about Germany and its defeated allies, but the spirit of cooperation was quickly fading.

The dominant role that the United States asserted in Europe gave the Soviets a reason to fear isolation from the West. They felt their future security depended on establishing a belt of pro-Soviet nations around their country. The West watched with alarm as communism took hold in several Eastern European countries. Free elections in Poland and Romania were never held, and in Hungary and Czechoslovakia, elected leaders were overthrown by Soviet-backed communists. In 1946 Stalin declared that capitalism was a threat to world peace and proceeded to expand Soviet military forces.

The Iron Curtain Is Drawn

The former allies were dividing Europe into two camps. In Fulton, Missouri, soon after Stalin's declaration, Churchill described the di-

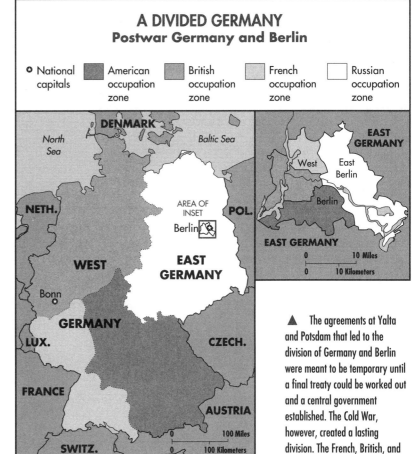

A DIVIDED GERMANY
Postwar Germany and Berlin

- National capitals
- American occupation zone
- British occupation zone
- French occupation zone
- Russian occupation zone

DENMARK
North Sea
Baltic Sea
NETH.
POL.
AREA OF INSET
Berlin
WEST GERMANY
Bonn
EAST GERMANY
GERMANY
LUX.
CZECH.
FRANCE
AUSTRIA
SWITZ.
100 Miles
100 Kilometers

EAST GERMANY
West Berlin
East Berlin
Berlin
EAST GERMANY
0   10 Miles
0   10 Kilometers

▲ The agreements at Yalta and Potsdam that led to the division of Germany and Berlin were meant to be temporary until a final treaty could be worked out and a central government established. The Cold War, however, created a lasting division. The French, British, and U.S. zones of Germany and Berlin were formally unified in 1949 into West Germany with its capital in Bonn. The Soviet zone became East Germany with its capital in East Berlin.

vision in concrete terms: "From Stettin in the Baltic to Trieste in the Adriatic, an iron curtain has descended across the continent."

The Cold War had begun in earnest not long after the real war ended. To many Americans, the spread of Soviet influence in Europe signaled a danger to the whole free world. Led by President Truman, the United States began to exert greater influence in affairs outside its own hemisphere. The agreements at Yalta and Potsdam failed to prevent the Soviets from controlling Eastern Europe, but Truman was resolved that communism should extend no further. When the Soviet Union stepped up supplies to communists in Turkey and Greece, the United States

U.S. NEWS REPORTS TO COMMUNIST WORLD

The Cold War was also fought over the airwaves. To counter state-controlled radio and television broadcasting in Eastern Europe and the USSR, the U.S. government supplied its own information to people in these countries. Many in the East came to rely on Radio Free Europe, Radio Liberty, and the Voice of America for news. Radio Moscow broadcast to the West as well.

countered by giving money and support to the governments of both countries. The Truman Doctrine, as this policy of support was called, became part of a strategy of "containment" that molded U.S. foreign relations for many years to come (see The Nation).

The United States also worked to make the West stronger through the European Recovery Program, or Marshall Plan (named for Secretary of State George C. Marshall). Begun in 1947, the plan gave money to European countries to help them rebuild their war-torn economies. Although the plan served several purposes, it was designed to stop the spread of communism. This led Stalin to call the plan "a capitalist plot" (see "European Economic Recovery").

The Tension Increases

One focal point of the Cold War was Germany. In 1948, the United States, Great Britain, and France announced a plan to unite their

zones of Germany, including the western zones of Berlin, by using a new form of currency among them. This plan did not include the areas controlled by the Soviet Union. Seeing this development as a threat, Stalin ordered the closing of all the highways and railroads that connected West Berlin with West Germany. He hoped to drive the Allies from West Berlin by sealing it off from food, fuel, and other necessary supplies.

The United States and other countries responded with a massive airlift of supplies to West Berlin. Over the next ten months, nearly 280,000 flights delivered over 2 million tons of supplies to the city. In the face of such resistance, Stalin finally backed down and lifted the blockade. The crisis strengthened ties between the United States and the new country of West Germany.

The growing mistrust of the Soviets led the United States and Western Europe to create their first peacetime military alliance. During the Berlin blockade, the United States, Canada, and ten European countries formed the North Atlantic Treaty Organization (NATO). This treaty ensured that if one partner were attacked, the others would come to help. With its strong economy and control of the atomic bomb, the United States took a dominant position in the alliance. In 1955 the Soviet Union secured a military alliance with six Eastern European nations through the Warsaw Pact.

Other changes increased fears in the West. The Soviets exploded an atomic bomb in 1949. That year, the communist takeover of China

▼ After the Soviet Union banned all land and water traffic between West Germany and Berlin, the United States, Great Britain, and France organized the Berlin airlift to get supplies to West Berlin.

made it a new factor in the Cold War. Chinese troops entered the Korean War in 1950 to help North Korea, which was already receiving Soviet aid. To the United States and its allies it seemed that Asia was becoming a huge communist bloc. In reality, Soviet and Chinese leaders distrusted each other.

The Rise of Khrushchev

When Stalin died in 1953, the rest of the world watched the USSR closely. After a power struggle within the Communist party, Nikita Khrushchev rose to the Soviet leadership in 1955. He was critical of Stalin's rule, and he took steps to improve relations with

Nikita Khrushchev: A New Spirit in Soviet Leadership

◄ Soviet premier Nikita Khrushchev (left center) and Vice President Richard Nixon debate the merits of their respective countries as they tour the U.S. exhibit in Moscow's Sokolniki Park on July 24, 1959.

anything else, he was driven to prove that the Soviet system was better than that of the West.

Khrushchev traveled to every corner of the USSR and to many countries around the world to observe and learn. He was the first Soviet leader to visit the United States, and his visit helped thaw the Cold War. But he never hesitated to criticize American society.

"We must build houses so they can be lived in by our children and grandchildren," Khrushchev once said to Vice President Richard Nixon. Nixon replied that future generations might have different needs and tastes. "Well, let them change the furniture," Khrushchev replied. "Why change the house?"

"We will bury the enemies of the Revolution," Soviet premier Nikita Khrushchev declared defiantly on a visit to the United States in 1959. The next day the headlines read: KHRUSHCHEV SAYS THE SOVIET PEOPLE WILL BURY THE PEOPLE OF THE UNITED STATES OF AMERICA!

Khrushchev never hesitated to say what was on his mind, and it was not the only time the press would take advantage of his candidness. When Disneyland refused to admit him into the park be-

cause of the security risk, he was irate. His words made the front page.

Khrushchev could roar one moment and smile the next. A complex and colorful leader, he had little formal education. He had risen from the Russian coal mines to the leadership of the Communist party and the USSR. Once in power, Khrushchev denounced his ruthless predecessor, Joseph Stalin. He began to reach out for "peaceful coexistence" with the United States. More than

Washington. Khrushchev and President Eisenhower held a **summit** meeting at Geneva, Switzerland. Khrushchev also visited the United States.

But if the Western nations had hoped the new Soviet leader would lift the Iron Curtain, they were disappointed. In 1956 a popular revolt in communist Hungary was brutally put down by Soviet troops. A wall went up between East and West Berlin in 1961. The Cold War continued to be waged all over the world, as the two superpowers tried to win over struggling **Third World** nations through political influence and economic aid. Through the 1950s and 1960s, both sides expanded their military presence worldwide and continued to stockpile nuclear weapons.

Hungarians Flee Repression

In 1949 Mátyás Rákosi became the communist ruler of Hungary. Supported by the Soviet Union, his command inflicted terror on the country and its people. After Stalin died in 1953, Rákosi was replaced by the more liberal Imre Nagy and political conditions improved. But Rákosi regained power two years later, only to reinstate his harsh policies. He resigned for good in July 1956, but the communist government remained resistant to reform.

Meanwhile, bitter resentment was building among the Hungarian people. Led by demonstrating students, a revolt finally broke out in October 1956. Soviet troops quickly moved in. Although Hungarian "freedom fighters" battled Soviet tanks with homemade bombs, the revolution was put down within a month. As a result of the uprising, more than 200,000 Hungarians fled the country. More than 30,000 came to the United States.

THE NEW FACE OF CHINA

The end of World War II began the final stage of one of the principal struggles of the twentieth century—the civil war in China between the Nationalist government and Chinese Communists. This upheaval involved more than a quarter of the world's population and led to the creation of a new communist nation, the People's Republic of China.

The civil war was fought between two rival political groups, the Nationalists and the Communists. The roots of this conflict went back to the overthrow of the emperor of China in 1911. The Nationalists, led by Sun Yixian (Sun Yat-sen), established a republic and introduced political and social reforms, but they found it difficult to hold the vast and ancient country together.

The next ten years were chaotic for China. The weak central government came under military control, and it had to battle with powerful regional rulers for domination. During this time, Chinese reformers were splitting into two camps. The Nationalists regrouped under Sun. A more radical group of Chinese, influenced by the recent revolution in Russia, formed their own Communist party. These Communists soon agreed to join forces with the more powerful Nationalists to unify China and pave the way for change.

With the aid of the Communists, the Nationalists began establishing control over the country. But the alliance between

Nationalists and Communists was never very solid. The successor to Sun, Jiang Jie-shi (Chiang Kai-shek), wanted to maintain firm control of the Nationalist party. He was wary of the Communists' beliefs and their numbers, which had grown from only 500 in 1925 to over 58,000 by 1927. He began to force them out of his government.

Jiang's administration contributed greatly to the rise of the Communists' following. He put up with widespread corruption and did little to improve the lives of China's millions of peasant farmers. He also relied heavily on his army to maintain order and limit opposition to his rule.

The alliance with the Communists came to a bloody end in 1927. Jiang's troops massacred thousands at a workers' protest that Communists had organized in Shanghai. Blaming the confrontation on the Communists, Jiang ordered a purge to get rid of them. In the "White Terror" that followed, Communist party members were shot on sight; more than 100,000 people were killed. The Communists fled to the countryside of southeastern China, where Mao Ze-dong (Mao Tse-tung), the son of a farmer, emerged as their leader.

Civil War and the Long March

The Communists' forced exile to the countryside focused their attention on the needs and conditions of the rural peasants—a major part of China's huge population. This turned out to be the Communists' greatest strength. From 1927 to 1931, Mao gained control of more than 15,000 square miles, and his

peasant following swelled to more than 9 million people. He also organized the Red Army, which included 300,000 soldiers.

Jiang continued to battle the Communists. In 1934, his armies surrounded the Communist center in the southeast. The Communists were forced to move out, and they started a long trek across China. In a year, the "Long March" took them over some 6,000 miles and across 15 rivers and several mountain ranges, with the Nationalists in pursuit. Thousands died along the way of exhaustion, hunger, and thirst. Of the 100,000 or so who began the march, only a fraction had survived when it ended in northern China. But the legendary march solidified Mao's party leadership and inspired many people to join his side.

When the Japanese invaded China in 1937, the attack put a temporary halt to the civil war. Once again, the Nationalists and Communists joined ranks, this time to fight the Japanese. During World War II Mao's position was greatly strengthened. The Japanese nearly destroyed the Nationalist Army, which saw most of the front-line fighting. Mao was able to gain control of large parts of the interior of China, changing local governments and creating land reforms in these areas. He was also able to turn patriotic feelings for the war into support for his party. After the Japanese were stopped, the civil war resumed.

At the end of World War II, the United States sent George C. Marshall (who later became secretary of state) to help Mao and Jiang negotiate a peace settlement between them. Neither side was willing to compromise, and Marshall's mission failed. The United States and its allies were concerned that the most populous nation in the world would fall into the hands of the Communists, and they believed that the Soviet Union was backing Mao. The United States began sending billions of dollars to support Jiang.

The Red Army continued to gain strength, however, and by 1948 it equaled Jiang's forces. In May 1949, the Communists had almost completely defeated Jiang's Nationalist army. Jiang fled to Formosa (now Taiwan), an island off the coast of China. In October 1949, Mao announced the birth of a new nation, the People's Republic of China.

Mao Ze-dong: The Builder of Modern China

As a boy growing up in China's Hunan province at the turn of the century, Mao Ze-dong was often found poring over books on geography, history, poetry, philosophy, and Greek mythology. Mao would use the thoughts and ideas he learned to develop his communist ideals.

By the time Mao left Beijing (Peking) University in 1919, he was already politically active. Two years later, he was a founding member of the Chinese Communist party. He worked to organize China's rural peasants, whom he saw as the key to change. Indeed it was the strength of the peasants supporting the Communists' military forces that helped the revolution finally to succeed. This success did not come easily, however.

On a cold day in October 1934, Mao was forced to flee from his headquarters in Kiangsi province with 100,000 of his followers. They included his second wife (his first wife had been executed by the Nationalist army), his children, his brother, and many friends. The Long Marchers set a fast pace across difficult terrain with Jiang Jie-shi's army at their heels. To stay ahead of the Nationalists, the marchers had to abandon their children. Mao himself left three of his children with peasants along the route. He never saw them again.

Mao often used poetry to recount the struggles of the revolution, project himself as its hero, and rally support among the peasants. In "Return to Shaoshan" he wrote,

> Many sacrifices, many strong wills,
> Will surely change sun and moon into a new sky.
> Happy to see waves after waves of paddy and beans.
> Everywhere heroes moving down through the evening mist.

Mao also put his military tactics in a simple poem:

> The enemy advances, we run away;
> The enemy camps, we harass;
> The enemy tires, we attack;
> The enemy retreats, we pursue.

After the revolution, Mao continued to write poems and slogans to encourage the Chinese people to follow his principles. His sayings were collected in *The Thoughts of Chairman Mao*, known as "the little red book." Mao's writings would influence people in China and other parts of the world for years to come.

The People's Republic

Mao had ambitious plans for his nation, and he faced many problems—both old and new. The turbulent years since the fall of the emperor had brought little change to the inequalities of traditional Chinese society. City merchants prospered from foreign trade, while rural peasants eked out a living working for large landowners. China also had to be rebuilt after long civil and international wars. Industry and agriculture needed to be modernized. Mao worked quickly to centralize control and overturn thousands of years of Chinese history.

The changes did not come without violence. Mao eliminated the control of the large landowners by seizing their land and spreading it among 300 million peasants. As many as 3 million people—primarily landowners—were killed. These executions were used to ensure support for Mao's leadership and his communist reforms.

Mao moved to put China's whole economy under state control. Borrowing a concept from the Soviets, he developed "Five-Year Plans" as blueprints to run the country. The first Five-Year Plan, begun in 1953, called for the expansion of industry under state ownership and the organization of group farms, called "collectives." Mao saw these collectives as a way to employ the peasants, while discouraging private ownership and increasing state control over farm production.

These collectives showed a few signs of success, but overall Mao felt their progress was too slow. He tried to speed it up through a second Five-Year Plan begun in 1958, which he called the "Great Leap Forward." The Great Leap was too much too fast, however, and it nearly destroyed the Chinese economy. After a year, the Great Leap Forward was declared a failure. Its breakdown was a blow to Mao's prestige, but he maintained control over the Communist party and the country.

▲ Victorious Communist troops roll into Shanghai in 1948, two years after full-scale fighting had resumed between Nationalists and Communists in China. Their banner depicts Mao (right) and Jou En-lai (Chou En-lai), a veteran of the Long March who would become the first premier of the People's Republic.

EUROPEAN ECONOMIC RECOVERY

Adolf Hitler had once said, "We may be destroyed, but if we are, we shall drag a world with us—a world in flames." His prediction came true, especially for Europe. From France to Russia, the war demolished thousands of farm villages. Cities and factories lay in ruin from the bombing campaigns of both sides.

demands for independence resumed and grew louder. The recovering economies of Europe had to deal with changing overseas markets.

Postwar Boom

To help themselves rise from the rubble, European countries were eager for economic aid. They looked first to the United States, which had kept the Allies supplied during the war. In 1947 the United States responded with the European Recovery Program, or Marshall Plan, a huge program of aid for Europe. The plan called for the countries who participated—17 in all—to direct and coordinate it. This left the government of each nation free to steer U.S. grants and loans into the industrial and agricultural areas most in need of help.

The Marshall Plan had a major impact on European economic recovery and expansion. In spite of some **inflation,** the recovery was remarkable. By the early 1950s, industrial output in Western Europe had risen to 35 percent above pre-war levels, and agricultural output was up 10 percent. As was the case in the booming United States, the economic expansion continued through the 1960s.

One side effect of the plan was the new sense of cooperation that it developed. Trade increased across Western Europe and between Europe and the United States. American industry also benefited greatly from the Marshall Plan. In exchange for the money offered as aid, participating countries bought many of the raw materials, machinery, and tools they needed from the United States.

▲ After World War II, factories such as the Krupp works at Essen in Germany lay in ruins from massive Allied bombing.

Millions of people were homeless and hungry. Both the winners and the losers had spent enormous amounts of money and resources mobilizing for war. The economy of Europe was in shambles.

The war had created confusion in European capitals as well. Many governments were uprooted before and during the war by the occupation armies of Nazi Germany. These governments had to regroup while their people struggled to recover and rebuild. The collapse of the losing countries—Germany, Austria, and Italy—left them without constitutional leadership. These and other weakened countries were managed by Allied armies until national governments could be formed.

The countries of Europe that had been dominant world powers were now badly in need of rebuilding. The global war also sped up the breakup of colonial empires. Across the African and Asian regions ruled by European nations,

Changes in Western Europe

In the years following the war, political changes were taking place in many Eastern European countries. Communist governments were taking power in the countries surrounding the Soviet Union. Communist political parties were also gaining popularity in some Western democracies, such as France and Italy. The United States was concerned that communism would spread through Europe if recovery took too long. This concern was the main reason the Marshall Plan was developed.

The Marshall Plan was not limited to U.S. allies. It was offered to all nations, even the Soviet Union, with certain conditions. Fearing the spread of American influence in Eastern Europe through U.S. aid, the Soviet Union quickly turned down assistance.

The Marshall Plan's success did help it to bring stability to several democratic governments. Employment levels and standards of living rose significantly in most of the countries that received aid. This made it difficult for communist parties to win majorities—workers were doing well. But **socialism,** which called for state ownership of some industries, did gain acceptance in postwar European governments. Many of them **nationalized** key industries and banks. **Social welfare programs** and state-supplied insurance became common throughout Western Europe. In many countries, especially in Sweden and other parts of Scandinavia, welfare programs became firmly rooted and their range began to grow.

A New Welfare State

The growth of the **welfare state** in Great Britain is a good example of this. Government control of resources and planning had been necessary for the country to survive during the war. At the end of the war, supplies were still limited. The British government continued to ration clothing until 1948, gasoline until 1950, and food until 1952, while the country recovered.

> *"Our policy is not directed against any country or doctrine but against hunger, poverty, desperation and chaos. Its purpose should be the revival of a working economy in the world so as to permit the emergence of political and social conditions in which free institutions can exist."*
>
> —George C. Marshall, address at Harvard University, June 5, 1947

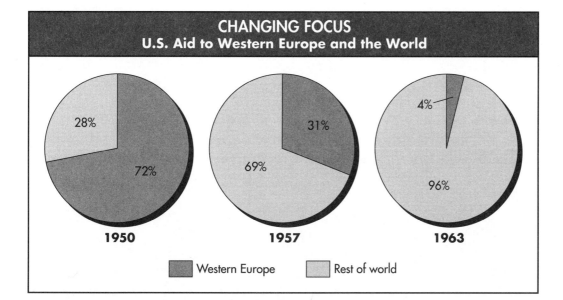

CHANGING FOCUS
U.S. Aid to Western Europe and the World

1950: 28% / 72%
1957: 31% / 69%
1963: 4% / 96%

Western Europe   Rest of world

◄ The Marshall Plan and other aid to Europe accounted for a large share of U.S. spending overseas in 1950. Once Europe was economically and politically secure, U.S. aid was channeled to Latin America and other developing areas.

"Two thousand years ago the proudest boast was 'Civitas Romanus sum' ['I am a citizen of Rome']. Today, in the world of freedom the proudest boast is 'Ich bin ein Berliner' ['I am a Berliner']. . . . All free men, wherever they may live, are citizens of Berlin. And, therefore, as a free man, I take pride in the words, 'Ich bin ein Berliner.'"

—John F. Kennedy, speech in West Berlin, June 26, 1963

In 1945 a socialist party, the Labour party, won a majority in the government. For the next six years, this party laid the foundation for a British welfare state by putting critical industries, such as coal mining, steel, and railroads, under government control. It also expanded social services. One major program was National Health Insurance, which guaranteed health care for all "from the cradle to the grave."

British recovery moved along more slowly at first than the recovery of some of its European neighbors. Most of its factories had survived the war intact, but many needed to be modernized. The breakup of the British Empire also required many economic and political adjustments. For the most part these changes were smooth, since most of the independent countries remained partners in the British Commonwealth.

De Gaulle's New Republic

France, which had been divided by Germany during the war, took steps to reseat its democratic government. In 1946 the French drafted a new constitution, which established the Fourth Republic. Guided by a combination of the Socialist and liberal Catholic parties, France made many economic and social reforms following the war. In a decade, it nationalized many banks, insurance companies, and industries. It also expanded welfare benefits.

Though the French economy was making steps toward recovery under the Fourth Republic, its government suffered from instability. A wide range of political parties—

from the Communists on the left to the Gaullists on the right—contended for a voice in government decisions. France was also finding it difficult to let go of its colonies.

The end of World War II did not mean the end of war for France. It continued to fight against independence movements in Southeast Asia and Africa. The French withdrew from Vietnam, Cambodia, and Laos in 1954, but a bloody war in Algeria, in northern Africa, continued. The French people became divided over what many saw as a pointless struggle. By 1958 France was at a crisis point.

The French turned to retired general Charles de Gaulle, a hero of World War II, to bring stability to the government. De Gaulle rewrote the constitution, establishing the Fifth Republic. The new constitution gave the presidency more power over the legislature, to strengthen the president's ability to determine policy. De Gaulle became president in December 1958. He put an end to the Algerian war in 1962 by granting the colony independence.

In foreign affairs, de Gaulle steered an independent course for France. He opposed the strong American position in NATO and began developing a separate nuclear weapons program. De Gaulle also established ties with Eastern European countries at a time when the gap between East and West was broadening.

Democracy Comes to the Axis

Both Italy and Germany charted new political and economic courses after the war. Democratic governments were established in both countries and both experienced spectacular economic growth.

In Italy, the fascist government that had been in place before the war was overthrown. A new constitution was adopted in 1947. In spite of many challenges from Socialists and Communists, the moderate Christian Democratic party dominated the government. Italy's industry boomed throughout the 1950s, aided largely by the Marshall Plan. Social reforms lagged behind Italy's economic change, however. By the early 1960s, the government was under pressure to solve many urban and rural problems.

In Germany—at least in part of it—democracy was given a chance to bloom. In 1948 France, Great Britain, and the United States agreed to merge their occupation zones to unify the western part of Germany. The Soviet Union organized a communist government in its zone. The separate countries of the Federal Republic of Germany (West Germany) and the German Democratic Republic (East Germany) were founded a year later.

In West Germany, the booming economy helped support a stable democratic government. Most German industry had been demolished in the war, but it was rebuilt from scratch with foreign aid. The new, modern factories of West Germany gave it a promising economic future.

Like Germany, Austria was divided into four occupation zones, which were not fully unified until 1955. At that time, the Soviet Union agreed to allow Austrian independence in return for huge pay-

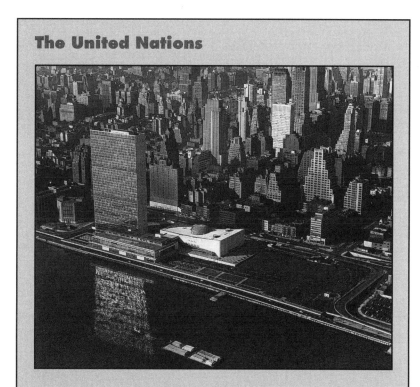

The United Nations

Planning for a new world organization dedicated to maintaining peace began with several Allied conferences during World War II. Fifty-one nations signed the United Nations Charter at the San Francisco Conference on June 26, 1945. The U.N. first met in London on January 7, 1946. In 1952 it established permanent headquarters on the East River in New York City.

ments in oil and cash. The long occupation took a heavy toll on Austria's resources, but by the time the troops withdrew, the country's economy was strong and its constitutional government stable.

INDEPENDENCE NOW

A chain reaction followed World War II. During the next 20 years, Europe's influence over the rest of the world toppled like a house of cards. Countries under colonial rule for hundreds of years used the crack in Europe's foundation to assert their independence. Anxious to gain independence and

Postwar Japan: Another Sunrise

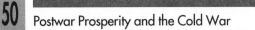 A year after the atomic bomb was dropped, Japanese children attend school in Hiroshima. Because of the lack of materials, none of the buildings had been reconstructed.

On the day of August 14, 1945, Japan's emperor Hirohito became a man. Until that day, many of his people considered him a god. But as a part of Japan's unconditional surrender at the end of World War II, Hirohito had to give up his claims to godhood and political power. The surrender also marked the first time in Japanese history that its people were controlled by a foreign government. An American general, Douglas MacArthur, was appointed supreme commander of the Allied powers (SCAP) for the occupation of Japan.

MacArthur's job was to keep the Japanese from making war again. He hoped to do this by having the Japanese adopt Western values. MacArthur and his occupation forces set out to change Japan's imperial government into a democracy.

They wrote a Western-style constitution, which was accepted by the Japanese Diet (legislature) in 1947.

One of SCAP's first steps was to remove the remaining military and business leaders responsible for Japan entering the war. Many "war criminals" were tried or purged. Emperor Hirohito escaped criminal treatment, partly because he was willing to cooperate with the occupation. Also, his religious importance and influence over the Japanese people prompted the Allies to keep him in power—but only as a symbolic leader.

The first two years after the war brought a surge of democratic reforms. New ideas about land ownership, education, and increased civil liberties changed the Japanese way of life. The occupation directed changes to all areas of society, including the press, the police, and private businesses. In 1947 MacArthur banned a labor union strike for fear that communism would take hold in the country. American involvement did mean that conservatives and business owners, some of whom had influenced the pre-war government, regained their power and wealth. Japanese business leaders set about to rebuild their economic empires.

Japan's economy, devastated by the war, rebounded quickly. It was given a boost by American involvement in the Korean War, which spurred Japanese industry. Japan continued to rebuild its factories with new machinery and modern technology, pointing its economy toward heavy industry and consumer goods.

American occupation ended when full self-rule was restored in April 1952. The Japanese government and economic structure had been marked with the thumbprint of American influence.

self-government, native peoples all over the world fought hard for independence.

Following World War I, **nationalist** sentiment began to flower across southern Asia, Africa, the Pacific, and the Middle East. Independence movements grew under influential leaders like India's Mohandas Gandhi and Indonesia's Sukarno. Two effects of colonialism—the spread of education and increasing **urbanization**—contributed to rising political awareness throughout colonial areas. After a second turbulent world war, the European powers, especially Great Britain and France, came under increasing moral pressure to give up their colonies. In some cases, the transition to independence went smoothly. In other cases, it was long and bloody.

Other factors contributed to the wave of freedom sweeping the globe. The United States pushed for an end to colonialism and recognized people's right to choose their own form of government. In 1947 the United States granted independence to its Pacific colony, the Philippine islands. The United States also wanted the colonies of other nations freed to open up new markets for American goods.

A Jewel Falls from the Crown

India's longstanding dreams for independence became a reality just after World War II. During the war, Great Britain first expressed its willingness to let go of its principal colony. The power of the Indian independence movement made freedom inevitable, but a huge roadblock to self-rule remained.

British India's two main religious groups, Hindus and Muslims, were at odds about whether India should be one independent nation or two. The Hindus, the majority in most areas, pushed for a unified India under Hindu control. The Muslims wanted a second nation to be carved out of Indian areas with Muslim majorities.

As the prospect of independence became real after the war, the internal struggle turned violent. A series of bloody religious riots took place throughout India. Hindu leader Jawaharlal Nehru and Muslim leader Mohammed Ali Jinnah finally agreed to divide the region. A new Muslim country—Pakistan—was to be created out of separate Muslim regions in the northwest and northeast. Hindus would control the rest of India. Pakistan and India became independent nations in August 1947.

The British withdrawal and transition was peaceful, but fighting continued between Hindus and Muslims. Much of the violence occurred during a mass migration of Hindus to India and Muslims to Pakistan. By 1948, some 13 million people had changed countries, and almost a million people had been killed.

On January 30, 1948, a Hindu fanatic assassinated Mohandas "Mahatma" ("great soul") Gandhi, the symbol of the Indian independence movement. This victim of violence had preached a philosophy of nonviolence that would influence political activists throughout the twentieth century. After Gandhi's death, Indians looked to Jawaharlal Nehru, their first prime minister, for leadership.

WOMEN GO TO THE POLLS

On April 10, 1946, women in Japan went to the polls to vote for the first time in the country's history. New constitutions in France, Italy, India, and China also gave women the right to vote in the mid-1900s.

Nehru led India through many challenges. One main task was to unify the huge new country, which had remained fragmented under centuries of foreign domination. A new Indian nation also had to overcome the rigid social structure of Hindu society and bring together hundreds of ethnic groups. Nehru oversaw the enactment of a constitution on January 26, 1950, and he led the world's largest democracy until 1964.

A Growing Global Forum: New U.N. Members, 1946-1963

Afghanistan	1946	Libya	1955
Albania	1955	Madagascar (Malagasy)	1960
Algeria	1962	Malaysia	1957
Austria	1955	Mali	1960
Benin	1960	Mauritania	1961
Bulgaria	1955	Mongolia	1961
Burkina Faso	1960	Morocco	1956
Burundi	1962	Myanmar (Burma)	1948
Cambodia	1955	Nepal	1955
Cameroon	1960	Niger	1960
Central African Rep.	1960	Nigeria	1960
Chad	1960	Pakistan	1947
Congo	1960	Portugal	1955
Côte d'Ivoire	1960	Romania	1955
Cyprus	1960	Rwanda	1962
Finland	1955	Senegal	1960
Gabon	1960	Sierra Leone	1961
Ghana	1957	Somalia	1960
Guinea	1958	Spain	1955
Hungary	1955	Sri Lanka	1955
Iceland	1946	Sudan	1956
Indonesia	1950	Sweden	1946
Ireland	1955	Tanzania	1961
Israel	1949	Thailand	1946
Italy	955	Togo	1960
Jamaica	1962	Trinidad & Tobago	1962
Japan	1956	Tunisia	1956
Jordan	1955	Uganda	1962
Kenya	1963	Yemen	1947
Kuwait	1963	Zaire	1960
Laos	1955		

Independence in Asia

After World War II, nationalist feeling that had long been building throughout European colonies in Asia reached a peak. Colonial rule had been disrupted by Japanese occupation, and independence leaders resumed their struggles to gain self-rule. Parts of the region became areas of particular concern for the United States, especially after the revolution in China in 1949.

Several British colonies followed the lead of India and Pakistan to gain independence after the war. Ceylon (now Sri Lanka), an island off the southern tip of India, was granted independence and became a member of the British Commonwealth in 1948. That year, Burma (now Myanmar) also gained independence from British rule. The British granted partial independence to Malaya, but they retained control over the country because of fear of a communist takeover. After a decade of internal strife, the British finally granted the Federation of Malaya (now Malaysia) full independence in 1957.

Another turbulent area was French Indochina, the area that now includes the modern countries of Vietnam, Laos, and Cambodia. Since the mid-nineteenth century, the French had colonized its rich mining and agricultural lands. The native peasants of the region worked long and hard to pay heavy taxes to the colonial governments. These peasants saw independence as a way to relieve their hardships. During the 1930s they began to back the Communist party, under the leadership of Ho

Chi Minh, who was leading the fight for Vietnamese independence.

Ho had worked for independence since the early 1900s. He had attended the Paris Peace Conference in 1918 to try to gain nationhood for Vietnam. The power vacuum left after World War II gave Ho the opportunity to achieve this goal. With France weakened from the war in Europe, he declared Vietnam's independence in 1945. The French wanted Vietnam, along with Cambodia and Laos, to accept independence under a new French Union, similar to the British Commonwealth. Ho would not settle for anything less than full independence for Vietnam, and war broke out between the French and Ho's army, the Viet Minh.

In 1954 the Viet Minh overran the French outpost in Dien Bien Phu, in northwest Vietnam. This battle marked the end of French control over the country. At a meeting in Geneva, Switzerland, representatives of several nations, including the United States, the USSR, and China, agreed to split Vietnam along the 17th parallel. The Western powers installed a government in the South, and Ho's Communists took over the North. Elections were to take place in 1956 to reunify the country.

Fearing the popular Ho would win, the South—at the urging of the United States—backed out of the commitment to hold national elections. The North began to organize Communists in the South into army units called Viet Cong. In the late 1950s, Viet Cong **guerrillas** began to attack villages in the South. In response, President Eisenhower began sending American military advisers to aid the South Vietnamese army. A new phase of the war in Vietnam was unfolding.

Changes in the Middle East

The global wave of independence spread over the Middle East, as well as in other parts of the world. Yet the region continued to be a hotbed of political, national, and religious clashes. Its strategic location and critical resource—oil—made it the focal point of many conflicts.

The most intense strife came over the creation of the nation of Israel. Jews in the Middle East and throughout the world had for centuries hoped for a Jewish homeland. The movement to create such a homeland, called **Zionism,** gained steam after the war. As the extent of the Jewish **Holocaust** in Hitler's Germany became widely realized, the idea of creating an independent Jewish state gained support worldwide. Israel declared itself a nation in 1948, and the United Nations recognized the Jewish government.

The new country was formed out of Palestine, the traditional home of Islamic and Christian Palestinians as well as Jews. The creation of a Jewish state there brought to a boil a history of conflict between Jews and Arabs in the region. For a time, the Soviet Union and Western nations found themselves on the same side, supporting the creation of Israel. But Arab Palestinians and neighboring Arab nations opposed the creation of a Jewish state and they joined forces to defeat the Israelis.

Israel: Birth of a Nation

Under the flag of the new nation of Israel, Prime Minister David Ben-Gurion (center left, with jacket), bids farewell to the last group of British troops leaving the region of Palestine. This marked the first time since 1918 that the Holy Land was free of British soldiers.

An independent nation was the dream of generations of Jewish people. That dream came true on May 14, 1948, when David Ben-Gurion—a leader of the Zionist, or Jewish nationalist, movement—signed Israel's proclamation of independence.

The Zionist movement was pushed forward by the 1917 Balfour Declaration, in which Great Britain expressed its support for a permanent Jewish homeland in Palestine. After the Germans and Ottoman Turks were defeated in World War I, the League of Nations gave Great Britain a mandate over Palestine and directed the British to make plans for a Jewish state in that area. Britain did little to honor its mandate, wavering in the face of conflicting Arab claims. The situation was still unresolved at the beginning of World War II.

After the Balfour Declaration, Jews from the world over began to migrate to Palestine. The pace of immigration quickened after Hitler's persecution of German Jews began in the early 1930s. Growing Arab resentment of the spread of Jewish settlements led the British to put strict limits on Jewish immigration in 1938. Still, thousands of Jews streamed to the area, many entering illegally.

After World War II, Jewish leaders continued to press their case, but they still faced extreme opposition from Arabs. British policy was unable to deal effectively with struggles between Arabs and Jews. In 1947 the British government asked the United Nations to decide the issue of Palestine. The United Nations approved a plan to turn the region into two separate states—one for Arabs and one for Jews. Arab Palestinians rejected this resolution, and angry fighting embroiled the region in civil war.

As the British pulled out in 1948, the Jewish representatives in Palestine declared their independence. Surrounding Arab countries invaded the new state. Israel won the year-long struggle that followed, the first of many Arab-Israeli wars. More than 700,000 Arabs fled Israel for neighboring Arab states, and more than a million Jews were expelled from Arab countries. An Arab state under the United Nations was never created; Jordan absorbed the territory.

The joint Arab effort against Israel gave strength to a wave of Arab nationalism that had been awakening since the war. New Arab countries—Jordan and Syria—were formed after the war out of areas controlled by France and Britain. Strongly influenced by their Islamic religion, many Arabs looked to strong leaders who would assert Arab interests in the region and the world. Colonel Gamal Abdel Nasser of Egypt emerged as such a leader.

Nasser took command of Egypt in 1952, after a military overthrow of King Farouk. His goal was to have the government take over industry and modernize Egypt. An important part of his plan was a new dam on the Nile that would provide electricity. Nasser gained U.S. support for the Aswan High Dam project, but the United States withdrew its loan in 1956 after Nasser made an arms deal with the Soviets. Nasser then seized the Suez Canal, a vital link in world shipping. Great Britain and France invaded Egypt to reopen the canal. The Suez crisis raged during several months in 1956, during which Israel joined the attack on Egypt. President Eisenhower asked for a U.N. resolution to stop the conflict. The United Nations gave Egypt the right to manage the canal.

During the Suez crisis, Arabs everywhere supported the man who stood up to the former colonial powers. Lebanese president Camille Chamoun was the only Arab head of state who refused to break ties with France and Great Britain. Although Lebanon had been predominantly Christian under French rule, by the mid-1950s

▲ Egyptian premier Gamal Abdel Nasser greets Muslim children in 1956. He was making a ceremonial visit to the tombs of Arab soldiers who died during fighting in Palestine in 1948.

it had absorbed many Islamic Palestinians from Israel. Palestinians and other Arabs, joined by leftist Christians, revolted against Chamoun's government in 1958. The resulting civil war was put down by U.S. Marines.

In Iran, nationalists who wanted to gain control of oil production successfully overthrew the country's king, Reza Shah Pahlavi, in 1953. The shah was strongly supported by the West because he allowed foreign countries to control Iranian oil. After the overthrow, Eisenhower feared communism would take root and the Soviets would gain control. American dependence on Iranian oil made this possibility a national threat, so Eisenhower asked the CIA to intervene. The shah was reinstalled as leader that year, and the future of Iranian oil for the West seemed secure.

A New Age in Africa

The twentieth-century borders of African countries had been drawn to suit the needs of the European

KHOMEINI EXILED

While Arab nationalism was gaining strength, winds of Islamic religious conservatism were also sweeping the Arab world. In the early 1960s, Ruhollah Khomeini became the spiritual head of the Shiites, a conservative Muslim sect in Iran. In 1963 he led a series of protests against the westernizing and modernizing policies of the shah. He was exiled from Iran in 1964. Khomeini returned to lead Iran in 1979 after an Islamic revolution overthrew the shah.

colonial powers. As European nations lost control over them, the new African nations found themselves with borders that made little sense to the native people. After colonial governments withdrew, these areas experienced internal strife among competing religious, tribal, and ethnic groups.

Names and borders in Africa changed frequently in the 1950s. African countries gained independence under a variety of conditions. During the 1950s, nearly all of northern Africa had gained its independence. Areas south of the Sahara were soon to follow. Ghana and Guinea took the lead, declaring independence before 1960. In the 1960s, the Belgians finally let go of the Congo, after a long, bloody fight. By September 1960, the United Nations had admitted more than 15 new African countries as members.

Like independence leaders throughout the world, most of the new African leaders had been educated in Europe. There they had learned Western ideas, and they therefore tried to establish Western forms of government. Most of the new leaders saw themselves as nation builders who wanted to modernize their countries. These goals were hampered by limited economic and industrial resources, so they often relied on assistance from the colonial powers they had overturned.

Self-rule did not become a reality for all black Africans during this era. Mozambique and Angola remained under Portuguese control until the 1970s. In other cases, white minority governments continued to rule where colonial governments left off. This was most notably true in South Africa, which had been an independent nation since 1931.

In 1948 a political party made up mostly of the descendants of Dutch settlers, called Afrikaners, gained power. The conservative Afrikaners were fearful of two things—a loss of white rule and communism. To avoid both threats, the South African government adopted a policy of extreme segregation known as **apartheid.** Blacks lived and worked in separate areas and had few political rights. The economic differences between blacks and whites were

▼ Between 1946 and 1963, 30 African nations gained their independence.

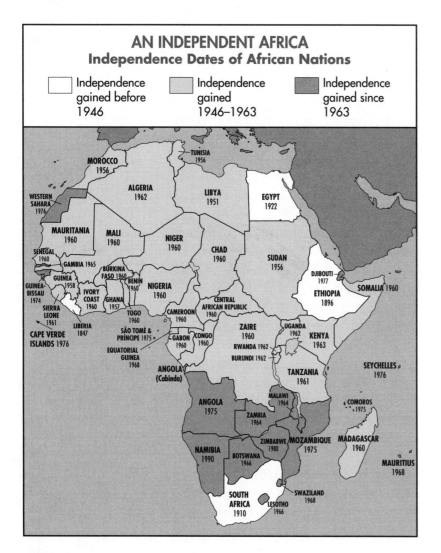

AN INDEPENDENT AFRICA
Independence Dates of African Nations

| Independence gained before 1946 | Independence gained 1946–1963 | Independence gained since 1963 |

severe even as South Africa's economy boomed in the 1950s and 1960s.

Despite international disapproval and pressure from the United Nations, South Africa brutally enforced apartheid. In 1960 police killed nearly 70 unarmed black protesters at Sharpeville, near Johannesburg. After the incident the South African government declared a state of emergency and outlawed black resistance groups, such as the African National

Jomo Kenyatta: The Father of Kenya

"Uhuru! Uhuru na Moja!" were the shouts that greeted Jomo Kenyatta in 1961, when he walked free after nine years in jails of the British colonial government. The eager cries meant "Freedom! Freedom and Unity!" Kenyans were shouting to the man they considered the father of their nation.

Kenyatta, of the Kikuyu people, was born around 1891 near Mount Kenya. As a boy he tended his father's sheep and made rounds with his grandfather, a rain-making magician. He saw white settlers spreading across his country, taking over land and turning proud people into second-class citizens. As a young man Kenyatta became involved in African nationalist movements.

Kenyatta decided that the only way to change things for the better would be to go to the source of his people's trouble—London. In 1929 he met with government officials in England to fight for Kikuyu land rights. Two years later he returned to London to continue his education. He stayed in Europe for 15 years, trying to influence the British government to reform its policies on Africa. He returned home again in 1946 to lead the independence movement there.

The struggle was not easy. The white colonial settlers believed that Kenyatta was the leader of the nationalist Mau Mau Society, which began a violent guerrilla uprising in 1952 against white settlers and the colonial government. Kenyatta protested his innocence, but the government jailed him.

During Kenyatta's jail term, the independence movement continued, and the British finally agreed to self-rule in 1960. After his release, independence and free elections followed quickly. Kenyatta became Kenya's first prime minister in 1963 and first president in 1964.

The Western powers were concerned that Kenya would become communist, but Kenyatta was very much against it. He said, "I've seen it and cannot be fooled. I know how it works." His anticommunist stand encouraged economic support from the West. Kenyatta also allowed the country's white settlers to continue dominating the country's economy. He felt that as long as the economy was strong, it would gradually make life better for black Africans.

Kenyatta typified the new African leader—born in Africa and educated in the West. He walked between these two worlds and managed to unify tribal people with many differences. He is remembered as a great African statesman and a voice for African unity.

APARTHEID

The word *apartheid* means "apartness" in the South African language of Afrikaans. It was the name given to the country's former policy of racial segregation based on white supremacy.

The apartheid laws guaranteed political control for whites, who made up less than a fifth of South Africa's population. They also severely restricted the rights of blacks to move about freely, form political organizations, hold certain jobs, and strike.

MANDELA

The African National Congress (ANC) was formed in 1912 to push for civil rights in South Africa. After the cruel apartheid laws were enacted in 1948, the ANC began to step up its efforts. Led by a group of young members that included Nelson Mandela, it urged its followers to oppose apartheid by any means, including violence.

Mandela was arrested in 1962 and charged with planning a revolution. At his 1964 trial he pleaded guilty, explaining that his people could win freedom only through violence. He was sentenced to life imprisonment.

Mandela was finally freed on February 11, 1990. Throughout his jail term he remained the symbol of democracy and majority rule in South Africa.

Congress (ANC). The divisive and destructive apartheid policy would dominate South African society for decades to come.

THE OTHER AMERICAS

Most Latin American countries had shed the yoke of colonialism before the twentieth century. Like other developing areas, however, these countries were not very industrialized. Their economies were still dependent on foreign trade. They relied mainly on their rich resources and agricultural products. In Central America especially, many of these were controlled by American and other foreign companies.

This dependence on foreign countries had given Latin America a history of political turmoil and severe economic problems. Latin countries were often run by harsh dictators, supported by the military and wealthy landowners. Great social inequalities existed. A good deal of Latin America's wealth went to foreign companies or into the hands of a privileged few. The middle class was growing, but much of the population still lived in extreme poverty. The Great Depression of the 1930s hit Latin America especially hard. These conditions made many countries ripe for change.

Latin governments changed several times over the next few decades. During and after World War II, a wave of popular uprisings toppled dictators all over Central America and South America. By

the late 1950s, some form of democracy had reached a majority of the region. Many of these new governments were unstable, however. In the early 1960s, several democratic governments fell again to military dictatorships.

Several underlying problems contributed to this instability. Latin America experienced a share of the wartime industrialization and postwar economic boom that occurred in other parts of the world. Greater prosperity helped more people reach the middle class, but the riches did not spread far. Big business and large plantation owners continued to get wealthy while their countries themselves were sinking into debt.

Prosperity also had its political effects. The rising middle class—educated and politically aware—began to use its greater numbers to press for democracy and social reforms. Many resented the cozy relationship between government and business leaders and foreign companies. They were sympathetic to the plight of urban workers, fruit pickers, and small farmers. The wave of democracy in the 1950s reflected the new political presence of the middle and lower classes. But attempts to reform land ownership or take over businesses usually ran head on into those who profited from them. These powerful interests—backed by military leaders, American companies, and sometimes by the American government—moved to retake control.

Yankee Go Home

Bolstered by the Monroe Doctrine of the 1820s, the American government had long asserted great influence over its southern neighbors. U.S. troops intervened in Latin America many times during the period between the late 1890s and the 1930s. They propped up failing governments and helped topple others. Over time, U.S. interference grew increasingly unwelcome. In 1933 President Franklin D. Roosevelt tried to improve relations through a "Good Neighbor policy." Under it, the United States vowed to be the financial helper rather than the military bully of the Western Hemisphere.

Latin American instability and fears of communism after World War II changed the "hands-off" tone of the Good Neighbor policy. In 1947 the United States renewed its option to use its armies in the Western Hemisphere. The Inter-American Treaty for Reciprocal Assistance (the Rio pact) allowed the United States to bring military support only to those countries that requested or allowed it, as permitted under the U.N. charter.

The Organization of American States (OAS) was formed in 1948, in part to oversee the Rio pact. The OAS was meant as a forum to exchange information, to discuss matters of common interest, and to restrict meddling from other countries. One part of the OAS charter allowed the United States to intervene in order to keep "peace and security in accordance with existing treaties." Many times the United States used this clause as a reason to stay involved in the economic and political policies of its Latin American neighbors.

Presidents Truman and Eisenhower paid little attention to social conditions in Latin America. But in the 1950s the United States did take notice of the political changes in the region. The American government became concerned about the socialist policies of some reform-minded governments. It sometimes stepped in to protect American business interests and keep the governments from leaning toward communism. One such case was in the Central American country of Guatemala. Arbenz Guzman, the elected president, made attempts to change land ownership and sieze the property of foreign

Nobel Peace Prize Winners, 1946–1963

1946	Emily Greene Balch	American social reformer/ economist/peace activist
	John Mott	American leader of the Young Men's Christian Association
1947	American Friends Service Committee	———
	Friends Service Council	———
1948	Not awarded	———
1949	John Boyd Orr	Scottish nutritionist/educator
1950	Ralph Bunche	American statesman/U.N. official
1951	Léon Jouhaux	French labor leader
1952	Albert Schweitzer	German medical missionary/ theologian/musicologist
1953	George C. Marshall	American statesman/general
1954	Office of the United Nations High Commissioner for Refugees	———
1955	Not awarded	———
1956	Not awarded	———
1957	Lester Pearson	Canadian statesman/U.N. official
1958	Georges Pire	Belgian priest/humanitarian
1959	Philip Noel-Baker	English pacifist/diplomat
1960	Albert Luthuli	South African political leader
1961	Dag Hammarskjöld	Swedish statesman/economist/ secretary-general of the United Nations
1962	Linus C. Pauling	American chemist
1963	International Committee of the Red Cross	———
	League of Red Cross Societies	———

businesses. In 1954 the United States sponsored a military overthrow of Guzman and helped install a pro-American dictator.

Changing Tides in Mexico

Mexico also had its history of economic problems, social unrest, and U.S. intervention. But during the 1930s, Mexico began to come into its own. A powerful but progressive central government brought stability to Mexico and instituted reforms, including a takeover of foreign oil industries. In 1940 Manuel Avila Camacho became president and began a program of industrialization. This led to one of the world's most impressive economic growth rates over the next two decades.

The country's industrial development and overall prosperity, however, did not solve lingering social problems and contributed to some others. The differences between rich and poor became even larger. As Mexican industry grew,

Fidel Castro: Student of Revolution

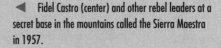

◄ Fidel Castro (center) and other rebel leaders at a secret base in the mountains called the Sierra Maestra in 1957.

Hidden in the mountains of Sierra Maestra, Fidel Castro and his rebel band faced death or glory. In 1957, rifles in hand, they were perched on the brink of a new way of life for all Cubans.

Those who knew young Castro never doubted that he would rise to greatness. In Castro's yearbook, his high school teacher and basketball coach wrote, "He has known how to win the admiration and affection of all.

He will make law his career, and we do not doubt that he will fill with brilliant pages, the book of his life."

A tall, serious young man with an athletic build and fire in his eyes entered the University of Havana Law School in October 1945. He later described the experience as more dangerous than his war against Fulgencio Batista. He never went anywhere on campus without a gun, which was not unusual for activist students at the time.

After graduation, Castro ran for the legislature. In March 1952, when Batista ended free elections, Castro took it as an act of war against the Cuban people. On July 26, 1953, Castro led a party of 123 men and 2 women in an attack on an army base in Santiago de Cuba. The rebellion failed, and Castro was jailed. Upon his release, he traveled to Mexico and America to build support for what he called the "26th of July Movement." Returning to Cuba in 1956, Castro and his followers retreated into the Sierra Maestra. There they began the guerrilla war that set off the Cuban Revolution.

so did its cities, and overcrowding and other urban problems became widespread. Mexico's population was also growing fast.

Upheaval and Crises in Cuba

Throughout the first half of the twentieth century, Cuba's fate was tied to the United States. Fulgencio Batista had come to power in 1934 with U.S. support. Batista left Cuba in 1944, but he returned in 1952 to reestablish his dictatorship. Batista allowed foreign business to develop industry in Cuba, but he ignored the poverty of most Cubans. His corrupt administration became the target of popular dissent and growing rebel movements. Successful guerrilla attacks on the government and resentment over Batista's actions helped the rebels win many supporters among the Cuban people.

By mid-1958 the rebels had completely disrupted Batista's government. The U.S. government stopped supporting him. Cornered, Batista fled to Spain on January 1, 1959. The leader of the rebel movement, Fidel Castro, assumed power in Cuba.

The United States watched with growing nervousness as Castro took control of its Caribbean neighbor. At first the American government was not sure in what direction he would take Cuba. Castro was openly critical of foreign influence—especially American—in Cuba. Relations became more uncertain when Castro assumed control of the landholdings of U.S. businesses in Cuba. The United States refused to sell Castro arms and urged its Western allies to do the same. In 1960 Castro turned to the Soviet Union for aid.

From that point, relations between the U.S. government and Castro worsened. Castro's actions had confirmed America's worst fears about him—that he was a communist.

The U.S. government took the threat of communism in Cuba seriously, and it set out once again to try to sway events there. Many upper-class and professional Cubans had fled to Florida when Castro assumed control. The CIA organized about 1,500 of these exiles and trained them for an invasion of Cuba to overthrow Castro. Planning began under President Eisenhower, and the invasion took place under President Kennedy.

Castro's army was waiting at Cuba's Bay of Pigs when the would-be rebels landed. The plan failed miserably, U.S. support was exposed, and 1,200 exiles were captured. Castro shut the door on all U.S. relations from that time forward. Shortly afterward, he declared, "I have been a Marxist-Leninist [communist] all along and will remain one until I die."

Castro strengthened his ties with Moscow, asking for more economic and military aid. In 1962 the Soviets began building bases for nuclear missiles on the island. When President Kennedy discovered this, he demanded that they be removed. For several days in October, the showdown between Kennedy and Soviet premier Khrushchev held the world in suspense. Eventually, Khrushchev backed down and removed the weapons. The United States has kept a watchful eye on Cuba ever since.

BUSINESS AND ECONOMY

In his September 6, 1945, message to Congress, President Truman turned his attention from America's victory in war to its economic future. Referring to the goals of the New Deal and GI Bill of Rights, he told the lawmakers, "Let us make the attainment of those rights the essence of postwar American life. After the First World War . . . we found ourselves in one of the worst inflations in history. We must be sure this time not to repeat that bitter mistake."

At first it appeared the United States was following the same path. The atomic bomb had suddenly ended the war, and 3 million jobs were lost within ten days after Japan's surrender. As mandatory price controls were lifted, prices skyrocketed. There were labor strikes and shortages of certain goods. It seemed that another economic crisis loomed ahead.

AT A GLANCE

- ▶ Full Speed Ahead
- ▶ A Consumer Society
- ▶ The Organization Age
- ▶ Blue-Collar, White-Collar
- ▶ Roads Across America
- ▶ The New Agricultural Revolution

Aided by government intervention, consumer demand, a strong industrial base, and technological advancements, the American economy quickly recovered. Businesses thrived and grew. As economic opportunities increased, Americans plunged themselves into their jobs and their families and enjoyed a new lifestyle. The Cold War world was unpredictable, but the material signs of success—big cars, well-furnished homes—helped preserve a sense of security.

By the 1950s, prosperity had become part of middle-class America's way of thinking. It confirmed many long-held beliefs in the promises the nation offered. During his 1952 campaign for president, Adlai Stevenson said, "The United States at mid-century stands on the threshold of abundance for all." Time magazine declared, "Easy Street now stretches from coast to coast."

DATAFILE

Wealth and productivity	1946	1963
Gross national product	$208.5 bil.	$590.5 bil.
Per-capita income	$1,264.00	$2,460.00
Trade balance		
Imports	$7.0 bil.	$26.6 bil.
Exports	$14.7 bil.	$32.6 bil.
Dow-Jones average	212.50	767.21
Raw steel output		
(short tons)	66.6 mil.	109.3 mil.
Auto factory sales	2.1 mil.	7.6 mil.

Labor force	1946	1963
Total	60.5 mil.	74.6 mil.
Male	72.2%	66.8%
Female	27.8%	33.2%
Unemployment rate	3.9%	5.7%
Union membership	15.0 mil.	17.6 mil.

Government	1946	1963
Federal spending	$61.7 bil.	$111.3 bil.
National debt	$18.2 bil.	$4.8 bil.

MARKET BASKET
Retail Prices of Selected Items, 1955

Bread (1lb.): **$0.18**

Three-minute phone call (New York to Denver): **$2.20**

Milk (½ gal., delivered): **$0.46**

Car (Buick Riviera): **$2,389.00**

Woman's dress: **$35.00**

Movie ticket: **$0.55**

Man's suit: **$90.00**

Hi-fi phonograph: **$200.00**

Postage (1st class, 1 oz.): **$0.03**

Electricity (per kilowatt hour): **$0.07**

Economy

FULL SPEED AHEAD

As America was changing from wartime to peacetime, businesses were confronted with uncertainty. Though long and terrible, the war had helped lift the American economy out of the Great Depression. Some economists predicted that a period of economic decline would follow the war, as it had after the First World War. The American economy did experience a period of painful adjustments, but the country that had fed and supplied the Allies during the war kept on producing after it. America's **gross national product** (GNP)—the yearly sum of all its production—grew steadily. Between 1945 and 1960, the GNP more than doubled, rising from $214 billion to $500 billion. By 1960, only 6 percent of the world's population lived in the United States, but it produced and consumed almost half of the world's goods and services.

One factor that kept the economy growing after the war was the beginning of a consumer spending spree. During the Depression, most people did not have enough money to buy the things they wanted. Consumer goods were scarce during the war, because so many of the nation's resources were used for war production. The end of the war unleashed a flood of buying and spending. Americans now had spending power, and after years of "doing without," they eagerly bought new houses, furniture, appliances, cars, and clothes. Construction companies could not build new homes fast enough to

"A climate favorable to business has been substituted for the socialism of recent years."

—Secretary of Commerce Sinclair Weeks, 1953

meet the demand. Makers of consumer goods profited from a booming market for new products, new brands, and new styles.

Government Management

The federal government took several steps to keep the economy from sliding back after the war. The GI Bill helped veterans and their families buy homes and go to college. The government sold the factories it had built during the war to private industry for $1 each; buying these modern plants so cheaply helped businesses convert more easily to peacetime production. Government bankers made credit more available for businesses to expand and consumers to buy. The government also continued to support farmers by buying excess food to keep prices up.

Widespread concern about unemployment prompted Congress to pass the Employment Act of 1946. The Employment Act gave the president and Congress new responsibility for overseeing the economy and boosting it when necessary to "promote maximum employment, production, and purchasing power." The Council of Economic Advisers was created to help the president make decisions about managing the economy. Through its goal of maximizing employment, the act permanently established an expanded role for the federal government in the economy.

The government also expanded its role more directly through increased spending. American businesses and their employees benefited from spending on new roads, schools, and housing, and on foreign-aid programs. The Cold War accounted for a whole new level of expenditure for defense. In addition to weapons production, government money poured into "research and development" ("R&D")—to find military or other uses for scientific discoveries and new technologies. Money also went into atomic research and, in later years, into the space program. Continuing a trend that began during World War II, government funding supported at least two-thirds of the R&D conducted in America during the late 1940s and 1950s.

By the time Eisenhower took office in 1953, the goals of the Employment Act—keeping the economy stable and unemployment low—had become established policy. Under this policy, government economists relied heavily on federal spending as a tool for managing the free market. Although the American economy continued to grow during the 1950s and into the 1960s, the federal government's new role was a mixed success. Unemployment continued to be a problem and federal budget deficits began to mount. **Recessions** in 1949, 1953, and 1958 temporarily slowed the economy. But for better or worse, the pattern of increasing federal spending had become a built-in feature of the marketplace.

Products of a Booming Economy

The other story of the postwar boom is the growth and changes in American industry. As factory production expanded, it continued to spread from its historical center in the Northeast throughout the country. The government spread production around during the war, and, as a result, many newly built war plants were located in the South and West. The rise of industry in these areas sped up the migration to the "Sunbelt"—the South and Southwest. Many urban areas in southern and western states grew quickly. Many old industries moved to the Sunbelt because labor and other costs were lower. The Sunbelt also became a center for newer industries, such as defense and space.

More changes came from technology developed during and after the war. Electronic computers were invented during the war, and by the mid-1950s, their presence was revolutionizing many businesses. Factories began developing and employing more automation on assembly lines and in other work areas. The rise of automation contributed to a rise in labor productivity (how efficiently workers do their jobs). More highly developed machines meant that factories could produce more and better goods with fewer hands.

An urban, more educated workforce also did their jobs better than ever before. Higher productivity allowed companies to pay their employees more without increasing prices. The workweek became shorter for many factory and office employees, giving these Americans more leisure time.

One of the most significant changes in the postwar economy was the dramatic growth of service industries. Their rise reflected Americans' rising standard of living, more urban lifestyle, and increased leisure time. Industries such as insurance, banking, communications, transportation, and

sales boomed, along with industrial production and consumer spending. Government services grew rapidly as well. Expanding federal, state, and local governments needed more office workers, teachers, social workers, and police officers. America was shifting to a service-based economy.

The service sector employed many of the swelling ranks of college graduates educated through the GI Bill. Most working women had service or office jobs. By the 1950s, workers in service industries for the first time outnumbered those in manufacturing.

Lost in the Change
In the midst of the rising GNP and standard of living, the economic changes that were taking place did not benefit everyone. While economic gains were widespread, they were also uneven. The income of whites grew much faster than that of blacks in the 1950s. More people reached the middle class, but

▲ While technology was transforming old industries, new developments, like television, created whole new industries. Workers at an RCA plant in Camden, New Jersey, test new television sets in 1950. More than 7 million sets were manufactured by RCA and other U.S. companies that year.

NEW WORDS
automation
compact car
computerize
"bread" (money)
windfall profit

the boom did little to lift up the poorest Americans in inner cities and rural areas. Furthermore, by the late 1950s, automation was eliminating hundreds of thousands of manufacturing jobs each year. The service sector absorbed some of these workers, but because service jobs generally required more education, many blue-collar workers felt themselves threatened by technology and progress.

Environmental concerns were also largely ignored during this period of expansion and prosperity. Air and water pollution, overuse of land and forests, and other environmental hazards were scarcely considered in the headlong rush toward economic growth.

MEDICAL INSURANCE: PRIVATE VERSUS PUBLIC

The American Medical Association (AMA) and the Truman administration butted heads over what type of health insurance the nation should have. Truman was in favor of a national insurance plan sponsored by the federal government. The AMA, representing the nation's physicians, favored voluntary private health insurance. The AMA argued that national health insurance would compromise the quality of medical care.

The AMA's great influence in Congress rebuffed several attempts to nationalize health insurance. In the 1980s the AMA changed its position to favor *some* form of national health insurance. Until that form is worked out, however, the United States will remain the only leading industrial nation in the world without a general national health insurance program.

Consumers

A CONSUMER SOCIETY

The end of the war began a new era of consumer spending. By 1950 the buying drive had reached high gear. Consumer spending over the next decade rose 38 percent, or twice as fast as the soaring population. As people made more money and felt more secure in their jobs, they began to expect more out of life. Wage earners could easily meet their families' basic needs. They now had the time to spend on leisure and the money to indulge in luxuries.

The consumer spending spree accommodated the new lifestyle of suburban society. Home and family were important to suburbanites, and families spent more time together. After the hardships of the Depression and the upheaval of war, parents wanted to have the best for their children and for themselves. Moreover, families' needs and tastes reflected a mobile, highly urbanized society. People were exposed to new products through the mass media, in their schools, and in their neighborhoods.

Something for Everyone

Americans' rising expectations and income were met by an exploding array of consumer goods. It seemed that new products were being introduced every day or improvements were being made to old ones. Technological developments created new types of products, from wash-and-wear shirts to high-fidelity record players to microwave ovens. Electrical devices made it possible to accomplish household tasks faster and more easily. Electricity had reached even the most remote parts of the country, and with it electric ranges and refrigerators became commonplace, along with mixers, blenders, toasters, and televisions.

The needs and wants of middle-class Americans were shaped by their exposure to mass media of all kinds. Popular fiction in paperbacks and magazines often depicted glamorous lifestyles. Images of comfortable home life on popular television shows made having the material goods of that life more desirable. Suburban homemakers learned the musts of good cooking, decorating, and entertaining from women's magazines like *Good Housekeeping* and *Woman's Day*. Magazines for fashion, sports, and hobbies showed consumers the latest looks and innovations.

The wide audience of the mass media, especially television, could quickly turn new brands into household names. The new scale of retail distribution through large supermarkets and shopping centers exposed consumers to a huge variety of goods. Companies spent millions of dollars to research packaging and product names that would make their merchandise stand out on long store aisles.

It also became easier to spend. More than ever before, people purchased big items—cars, appliances, furniture—on the installment plan. Monthly payments to banks and department stores were a fixture in most middle-class budgets. Checking accounts were also becoming popular. Checks and charge accounts made buying on impulse easy.

Car Crazy

Nothing symbolizes 1950s consumerism more than the automobile. After the war, the demand for new cars was limited only by Detroit's ability to produce them. As automakers caught up with the market, they began to satisfy Americans' growing taste for luxury and improvements. Automakers encouraged people to think of cars less as transportation and more as a statement of style. Car models were revised every year, and each one promised to be bigger, sleeker, and faster than ever before. By the late 1950s, styling features became prominent—taillights turned into tail fins, and shiny chrome and bright colors covered the body. People traded in their cars for new models even before their cars got old.

The automobile played an important role in shaping the consumer culture of the suburbs. While suburban shopping centers, malls, and supermarkets sprang up, other businesses changed or arose to cater to automobile traffic. Banks installed drive-up windows. Drive-in movie theaters spread all over the country, offering families a night out—or teenagers a night on their own—in their cars.

Spreading the Word

To push old and new products in an increasingly complicated market, businesses devoted bigger budgets to advertising. This led to phenomenal growth in the advertising industry in the 1950s. Companies staked the success or failure of their products on huge campaigns. Advertising agencies turned out hundreds of slogans, jingles, and other imaginative and ridiculous creations to encourage people to buy. They found a captivated audience in television viewers. People stayed glued to their

AMERICANS WAKE UP TO HIGH COFFEE PRICES

Complaints about the rising cost of living always grow more urgent when inflation hits Americans where they drink. In 1954 the price of coffee rose sharply in the United States because Brazil, the leading exporter, raised its selling price. While coffee had cost the consumer, on average, about 89 cents a pound in 1953, it shot up to an average of $1.11 a pound in 1954. Some grocery stores reported selling the commodity for $1.35. Restaurants were forced to charge 15 cents rather than 10 cents for a cup. Yet coffee drinkers changed their habits only slightly. They went from consuming 17 pounds of coffee per person in 1953 to 15 pounds in 1954.

▼ Drive-in restaurants, where "carhops" served customers food in their cars, became the place to eat out and "hang out."

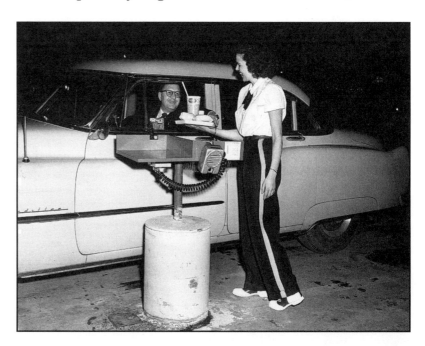

According to the U.S. Department of Agriculture, in 1963 the average American consumed 170 pounds of red meat, 37½ pounds of chicken, more than 300 pounds of milk and cream, about 9 pounds of cheese, 16½ pounds of butter and margarine, almost 17 pounds of apples and 22 pounds of citrus fruits, 18 pounds of ice cream, 318 eggs, and almost 16 pounds of coffee.

Today Americans eat less than 140 pounds of red meat a year, and they consume less milk and cream and eat fewer eggs. At the same time Americans now eat more than 70 pounds of chicken and 25 pounds of cheese each year.

sets while cigarette packs danced across their screens.

At the same time, advertising techniques were also becoming more sophisticated. Advertisers tried to appeal to Americans' awe of modern technology. They used scientific language to sell products, often promoting "advanced formulas" with scientific names. Advertisers also relied on so-called hidden persuaders—subtle appeals to a consumer's basic desires and fears. More than ever before, ads contained direct and indirect messages about how products would improve the buyer's status, popularity, health, or sexuality.

Consumer Society Critics

Another kind of consumerism was finding a revival in the late 1950s.

Spurred by books like Vance Packard's *The Hidden Persuaders* and *The Waste Makers*, some people began to question how products were promoted and sold. Packard and others criticized ads with hidden or misleading messages and encouraged consumers to wise up to advertising's persuasive power. Critics also noted a decline in the quality and durability of American goods. Some blamed manufacturers for deliberately designing merchandise to wear out quickly so more could be sold.

While social critics blamed business and industry for encouraging consumption and waste, they also found fault with the materialism in the values of the consumer society. They felt that Americans engrossed in consumption were unconcerned about social problems and ignored the by-products of their own comfort. In *The Affluent Society*, John Kenneth Galbraith described a typical suburban family out for a drive in their "air-conditioned, power-steered, and powerbraked automobile," passing "through cities that are badly paved, made hideous by litter, blighted buildings, billboards, decaying refuse." "Is this, indeed," Galbraith asked, "American genius?"

The Rise of the Golden Arches

McDonald's, number one in fast-food restaurants today, opened its first restaurant in December 1948. Owned and operated by Richard and Maurice McDonald, the restaurant was located in San Bernardino, California. In 1953 the entrepreneurs decided to build the now-famous pair of golden arches to catch the public's attention.

In 1954 the McDonald brothers were approached by Ray Kroc, who was selling a mixing machine. Kroc sold the brothers several of these machines for making milkshakes. Kroc also secured the right to franchise their operation. In 1955 Kroc opened his first McDonald's in Des Plaines, Illinois. Six years later, he bought out the McDonald brothers for almost $3 million.

Corporations

THE ORGANIZATION AGE

Charles Wilson, Eisenhower's secretary of defense and former president of General Motors, had once remarked that what was good for General Motors was also good for

Taking to the Highway: American Drivers and American Cars

During the conversion from war to peace, factories that had been used for making tanks and jeeps began producing Cadillacs, Chryslers, and Fords. And Americans were eager to buy them. Through the 1950s, suburban families began purchasing their second or third car. In 1950 the United States produced two-thirds of the world's cars, and by 1955 it was producing three-quarters. Two things were clear: Americans loved their cars, and the U.S. auto industry was on top of the world.

Most of America's cars came from Detroit's "Big Three"—General Motors, Ford, and Chrysler. Aided by defense contracts, highway funding, and expanding foreign markets, their profits soared and their corporate reach extended globally. By the mid-1950s, smaller car companies had been forced to combine in order to compete. Nash and Hudson, for example, formed American Motors in 1954.

The look and feel of cars were changing through the 1950s. Manufacturers added refinements such as power

steering and power brakes. Automakers saw higher profits in the market for larger cars, and they did all they could to get buyers to "trade up" to bigger models. Designers fashioned cars low to the ground, installed powerful engines, and added striking features. Yet their low profile allowed the slightest bump to smash the oil pan, muffler, or gas tank.

Detroit's emphasis on style over function had other drawbacks. Bigger cars guzzled gasoline and were more expensive to repair. They were often more dangerous as well. Some models, like the 1953 Buick, had inferior brakes. Tires were often not sturdy enough for heavier cars. Seat belts were an extra-cost option. Overall, considerations like safety, economy, and reliability were afterthoughts. Deaths on the

highways mounted to more than 40,000 a year by the late 1950s.

By the end of the 1950s some people began to change their ideas about cars. The new popularity of Germany's Volkswagen (VW) "Beetle" caused Detroit to think twice about its auto designs. The Beetle was small and economical. By 1957 almost 200,000 VWs had been sold in the United States. American auto manufacturers rushed to put out a small car. GM's first compact car was the Corvair, whose design was later found to be dangerous.

But the love affair with the big car was not over yet. Although American auto companies peaked on the world market in the mid-1950s, they still reigned supreme in the United States through the 1960s.

▶ Factory sales of cars, trucks, and buses shot up after the war and then followed the ups and downs of the economy. The dips reflect the recessions of 1952 and 1958.

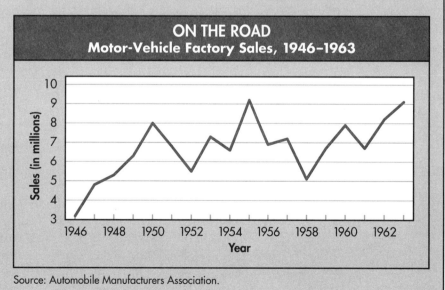

ON THE ROAD
Motor-Vehicle Factory Sales, 1946–1963

Source: Automobile Manufacturers Association.

On January 17, 1950, nine robbers held up an office of Brink's Inc. armored car service in Boston, Massachusetts. The thieves, wearing Halloween masks, made off with more than $2.5 million. This was the largest robbery to date in the United States.

Six years after the crime was committed, the FBI caught the fugitives, but only a fraction of the missing money was recovered. Eight of the robbers were sentenced to life in prison.

the country. Indeed the 1950s were good for big business. America's largest corporations benefited the most from the nation's prosperity, huge government contracts, and needy foreign markets.

A wave of business mergers followed the Second World War and continued to build throughout the 1950s and 1960s. Over this period, large companies acquired smaller ones at the rate of about 800 per year. Big companies continued to grow bigger, but a definite shift was taking place in how they grew. Through the first half of the century, mergers usually involved companies that produced the same things or supplied each other. During the 1950s, companies began to **diversify**; that is, they looked to buy other companies that made different products. Companies diversified to vary their operations and expand their product lines so as to protect themselves against economic slowdowns in any one area. Diversification also allowed companies to grow larger without appearing to monopolize any one industry.

Large diversified companies became a prominent part of the American business scene. American corporations also expanded their global reach in the postwar era. The value of U.S. exports doubled during the 1950s, reaching $20 billion a year by 1960. The value of overseas operations rose even faster. Firms such as the Ford Motor Company became truly **multinational,** with plants all over the world. After World War II, American corporations expanded into recovering European markets. Investment in Europe continued to

grow after the formation of the Common Market in the late 1950s, as U.S. firms tried to position themselves in the new economic system of Western Europe. New markets also opened up in emerging **Third World** countries.

Government spending, much of it stimulated by the Cold War, played a major role in the growth of corporations. As budgets for military and other research and development soared from the millions to the billions through the 1950s, so did the fortunes of the leading contractors. Government contracts also contributed to the diversification trend, as companies added new divisions for their work on defense or other technical areas.

The benefits for the large firms themselves were both direct and indirect. Government funds supported developments in electronics, computers, automation, chemicals, and medicine. Companies that did the R&D were on the cutting edge of these technologies. Their innovations contributed to new products that they could market and sell to consumers and other businesses. On the world market, American firms led the way in many of these areas for years.

The rise of government contracts had less-positive effects. The federal government made attempts to stimulate competition when awarding contracts, but a huge share of them went to a handful of large corporations. To some observers in the 1950s, large contractors, especially those in defense industries, were becoming too big and powerful. Many of these companies had a stake in keeping defense budgets high. The federal government and private business were becoming increasingly dependent on one another.

A few voices also warned about the merger trend and the increasing size of the leading corporations. Size gave these corporations more power to keep prices high. But amidst the overall economic growth of the 1950s, the trend toward bigness was seen by many as a necessary part of America's strength and dominance. Both liberals and conservatives saw its benefits. Liberal economist John Kenneth Galbraith, for example, argued that the power of big business was balanced by big labor unions, big government, and consumer pressure (although he would later reject this idea). As an illustration of how concentrated American industry had become, by the mid-1950s 23 corporate giants employed 15 percent of all workers in the manufacturing sector.

Corporate Management

Interwoven with the growing size of corporations was the new dominance of professional management. Throughout the twentieth century, the trend in big business had been one in which individuals or families transferred control to hired managers who acted on behalf of stockholders. The movement toward diversified and multinational firms during the 1950s sped up this trend. Operating far-flung companies with multiple divisions and thousands of employees required skillful executives and new managerial structures.

Modern corporations required managers to oversee commercial, government, and foreign departments and all areas of planning, development, design, marketing, and sales. As corporations grew, new ranks of middle management were added to the corporate structure. Businesses began to place more and more value on managers with degrees in business administration, such as the M.B.A. (Master of Business Administration). The science of business management was becoming ever more refined.

Corporate growth created many opportunities for secure and well-paying careers. As a generation of college-educated veterans and others flocked to the business world, they found themselves entering a new way of life. Advances in technology, new methods of doing business, and complex organizations meant that people entering large corporations had a good deal to learn before they could do their jobs. Companies ran training programs to teach new workers everything from how to answer the telephone and write business letters to how to dress. Companies also tried to establish a "corporate image" in their employees' minds and inspire devotion to the firm and its views.

Work

BLUE-COLLAR, WHITE-COLLAR

In the postwar economy, most American workers were experiencing changes. This was especially true for blue-collar workers—those in industry and other manual trades. Blue-collar workers shared the economic benefits of the 1950s

HOW TO SUCCEED IN BUSINESS

In the corporate culture of the postwar era, unwritten rules for looks, behavior, values, and even family life were commonplace. Men dominated all but the lowest levels of most firms, because they had the only real chance to move up the "corporate ladder" into managerial positions. Corporations valued men who could get along and fit in. Lured by an upscale lifestyle, many willingly conformed to corporate expectations.

Social critics found flaws in the corporate emphasis on conformity and organization rather than individuality. In *The Organization Man*, William H. Whyte summed up the corporate attitude as "a belief in the group as the source of creativity" and "a belief in 'belongingness' as the ultimate need of the individual." Whyte and other critics warned that while this belief served the goals of the organization, such thinking would create an America of followers rather than leaders.

▲ In the postwar era, automation increasingly controlled tasks in heavy industry once handled by human labor. These Ford pistons, for example, were automatically conveyed through the stages of the engine manufacturing process.

boom. Skilled and unskilled workers in manufacturing jobs began to earn enough money to purchase suburban homes and other tokens of middle-class life. Union workers made many great strides, securing fringe benefits such as insurance and pensions.

But blue-collar workers also had to adapt to changes in the workplace. Technology and automation were making some jobs easier, others more monotonous, and still others unnecessary. The modern workplace was more specialized and placed more value on education and training. The American worker had both a secure present and an uncertain future.

Loosening Labor's Hold

Nowhere were these conflicts more evident than in changes to labor unions in the postwar era. During the Depression, unions had grown in appeal and strength. The 1935 Labor Relations Act gave unions powerful new rights as to how they could organize and bargain with employers. Pro-business conserva-

tives complained that unions were becoming too powerful, and after the war others began to share their resentment. Conservatives blamed the unions for rising prices and shortages of certain goods. A wave of major strikes during 1945 and 1946 added fuel to their fire. Workers were as anxious as anyone to share in the postwar prosperity, and their unions demanded more money, shorter hours, and safer working conditions.

During the 1946 congressional elections, the problems of the postwar economy—**inflation,** shortages, and strikes—were a major Republican theme. After the GOP won a majority of seats in that election, the group set about to restrict the power of unions. The Labor-Management Act of 1947, better known as the Taft-Hartley Act, outlawed certain union practices and banned "closed shops," in which workers had to be union members to be hired. It also gave the American president the power to intervene in strikes that threatened national health or safety. Workers could be forced back to work for an 80-day "cooling off" period. Truman vetoed the act, but Congress overrode the veto. Organized labor called the law the "slave-labor act."

Unions Unite

Nevertheless, the Taft-Hartley Act had little immediate impact on the major unions. Unions held their own during the years that followed, as enrollment rose to new highs and union workers did well. Beginning in the late 1940s, workers in heavily unionized industries, such as steel, autos, and coal mining, gained favorable new contracts. For the first time, these contracts included automatic wage increases tied to the cost of living. They also included benefits for retirement, health, and disability.

Despite these gains, however, unions faced other challenges. Their growth had slowed substantially by the mid-1950s. They also faced an anti-union political climate. To cope with these problems,

Meany and Reuther: Captains of Labor

◀ George Meany (left) and Walter Reuther celebrate the merger of the AFL and CIO.

The merger of the American Federation of Labor (AFL) with the Congress of Industrial Organizations (CIO) in 1955 brought together two dynamic labor leaders, George Meany of the AFL and Walter Reuther of the CIO. The two men's careers reflected different aspects of the labor union movement. Reuther's background as an autoworker and industrial organizer in the 1930s was influenced by his involvement in left-wing politics. Trained as a plumber, Meany arose from the less-radical tradition of craft unionism.

George Meany was born in 1894, and as a teenager he started working as an apprentice plumber. Like his father, Meany became active

in the local plumbers' union. This was the beginning of a lifetime of work for organized labor. He held a series of posts in the AFL and became its president in 1953. One of his first steps as president was to revive reunification talks with the CIO.

Like George Meany, Walter Reuther followed the active unionism of his father. In 1927, at the age of 20, Walter left his home in Wheeling, West Virginia, to work in the auto plants of Detroit. During the Depression, Reuther worked to build the small autoworkers' union and was active in socialist causes. He also worked in the Soviet Union for a few years. Upon his return to the United States, he

became active in the United Auto Workers (UAW) union. His outspoken style, negotiating skill, and willingness to take risks quickly propelled him to the forefront of the sometimes violent UAW struggles of the 1930s. Reuther became president of the UAW in 1946 and president of the CIO in 1953.

As head of the larger AFL, Meany became president of the combined AFL-CIO. Although both Meany and Reuther were instrumental in the merger, they did not always see eye to eye. They did work together to employ the union's collective strength for bargaining and political action. They also fought corruption. The powerful Teamsters union was expelled from the AFL-CIO in 1957 for its connections to organized crime. Other disagreements built up, however, and Reuther eventually withdrew the UAW from the AFL-CIO in 1968.

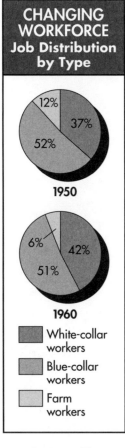

CHANGING WORKFORCE
Job Distribution by Type

1950
37%
12%
52%

1960
42%
6%
51%

■ White-collar workers

■ Blue-collar workers

■ Farm workers

▲ Two major workforce trends during the 1950s were the growth of white-collar employment and the dwindling number of farm workers.

two of the largest union organizations, the American Federation of Labor and the Congress of Industrial Organizations, reunited in 1955 to form the AFL-CIO.

The creation of the AFL-CIO signaled the arrival of "Big Labor" in the U.S. economy. Union leaders in this era began to seek better relations with corporate management, which they saw as a key to their own survival. They took a more businesslike approach in negotiations and in running their own organizations. The AFL-CIO had more power to win good contracts in more industries. But it also faced more public discontent about its size and power. Problems with corruption in some of its branch unions made this situation worse.

The Changing Workplace

At its peak in the mid-1950s, union membership included a third of all nonfarming workers. At about the same time, unemployment began to rise among blue-collar workers, the heart of unionism. The effects of automation, foreign competition, and other factors were beginning to be felt. Industrial companies continued to grow, but they needed fewer laborers and more white-collar (professional, technical, and office) workers. White-collar positions also dominated the fastest growing areas of the economy— service industries and federal and local governments.

The growth of public and private service jobs brought additional changes to the workplace. Cut off from manufacturing jobs after the war, women benefited the most from expansion in the service sector. Also, many service careers

required more education. As a result, more people than ever were going to college. College enrollment grew especially fast in such areas as advertising, education, social work, entertainment, and the arts. These fields were becoming more professional, more technical, and more specialized.

At the same time, the service-sector economy also created many low-paying jobs in cities. The demand for people willing to work for low wages drew many underprivileged minorities to urban areas as the white middle class was moving out. In search of new opportunities, blacks migrated from the South to the Northeast, Midwest, and West Coast; Puerto Ricans to the East Coast; and Hispanics to the growing cities of the Southwest and California.

Transportation

ROADS ACROSS AMERICA

Between 1945 and 1955, the number of cars on American roads had doubled to more than 50 million. Many roads in and around cities were clogged with traffic. People driving between urban areas or heading to vacation spots had to pass through the center of every town along the way. Pressed by the urgent need for better roads between and around urban areas, Congress passed the Interstate Highway Act in 1956. Construction of the coast-to-coast highway system was to become one of the most extensive public works projects ever undertaken in America.

Two-Lane Blacktop

The Interstate Highway Act authorized the building of a nationwide network of more than 40,000 miles of high-speed, limited-access freeways. These interstate highways were designed to accommodate a fifth of the nation's motor traffic, connect all continental U.S. states, and reach 90 percent of all U.S. cities of 50,000 people or more. Highway legislation passed in later years expanded the system several times. Officially named the National System of Interstate and Defense Highways, the project was also conceived as a defense measure to provide adequate routes for military traffic in times of emergency. To pay for the roads, Congress established the Highway Trust Fund, which was made up of federal money and special taxes on cars, gasoline, and other products. This fund contributed 90 percent of the cost of these roads; states supplied the rest.

Building the interstates injected money into a booming economy. The billions of dollars that were spent annually on the roads themselves benefited road construction companies and their workers. As highway building progressed, wider areas around cities became more accessible, and new suburbs sprang up. This spurred continued growth in suburban housing and business construction.

While the number of automobiles had made road construction necessary, the new interstates made having a car more necessary than ever. Most of the new suburban areas that grew up around the new highways were reachable only by car. By 1958 there were more

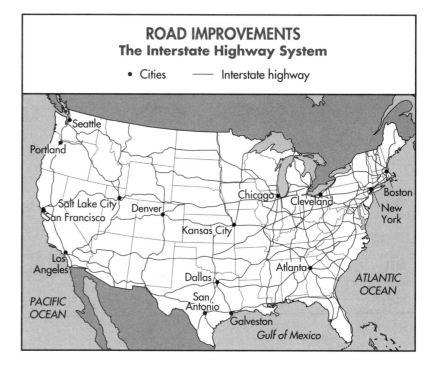

ROAD IMPROVEMENTS
The Interstate Highway System

• Cities   —— Interstate highway

▲ The interstate highway system as it was proposed in 1956 comprised a network of 41,000 miles, as shown on the map. By 1960 about 10,000 miles were open to traffic.

cars on the road than households in America. Nearly 12 million families, mostly in the suburbs, had two or more cars. The 1960 census reported that 65 percent of the working population drove their own cars to work.

Comings and Goings

While an adequate freeway system was necessary, the interstate highway program had its drawbacks. As it focused on highways, the federal government almost completely ignored planning and funding for public transportation. During the 1950s and 1960s, three-quarters of the federal transportation budget went to highways, while only 1 percent went toward urban mass transit. As state and city budgets followed this lead, rail and subway systems slid into decline.

Critics of this policy suggested that powerful "highway interests"—automakers, construction firms, and oil and rubber companies—lobbied hard to keep road

▲ Superhighways helped truckers and farmers. Wide and open roads and cheap gasoline made trucking increasingly economical for long-distance commerce. Trucks were quickly replacing railroad cars to transport everything from vegetables to manufactured goods to pre-fabricated houses. The interstates also made it easier and more economical for farmers to deliver crops to a wider market.

building a federal priority. Indeed, the Interstate Highway Act indirectly supported these interests at the expense of other forms of transportation. This imbalanced policy would contribute to the long-term problems of pollution and inner-city decay. Moreover, the urban traffic problems it aimed to solve would only grow worse.

Los Angeles, for example, had an extensive system of trolleys and rail lines before World War II. City leaders and highway interests, however, saw the car as the key to L.A.'s future. After the war, the system came under the control of a private company that began shutting it down completely. Some of the rail lines were replaced with bus routes, but the Los Angeles area became largely dependent on private automobiles. The city today is known for its congested freeways and smog.

In Los Angeles and many other cities, new highways changed the urban surroundings permanently. Roads cut through and redefined city neighborhoods. The "concrete

jungle" of elevated roadways, exit ramps, and parking lots became a prominent feature of the urban landscape.

Most drivers in the 1950s, however, were unaware of where these changes were leading. Interstate highways gave them speed, mobility, and freedom. Americans were eager to travel that next ribbon of highway.

THE NEW AGRICULTURAL REVOLUTION

Since the early part of the century, American farmers had benefited from better agricultural machinery and the applications of scientific breakthroughs in chemistry, genetics, and medicine. Advances in farming techniques after World War II were equally dramatic. A new agricultural revolution in technology and productivity hastened the trends of the previous 50 years. This technology was reducing the amount of land and labor needed for farming.

By the end of the war, nearly all American farms used machinery powered by gasoline or electric motors. Rural electrification programs during the Depression brought electricity to most farms. High food prices, high demand, and a shortage of labor during the war led many farmers to invest in modern equipment and try new methods.

A wealth of new products and techniques became available in the postwar years. New fertilizers, pesticides, and weed killers helped improve crop production. Farmers planted new varieties of grains and raised stronger breeds of livestock. The new strains were more productive and less prone to disease. More efficient equipment and new scientific techniques added to farm productivity and lowered the per-acre costs. The federal government sponsored agricultural research and development and helped spread information about new products and methods.

Modern farm machinery and techniques meant that fewer farmers could produce more food on less acreage. During the 1940s and 1950s, the number of farms in America decreased by a third, from 6 million to 4 million, while the size of the average farm nearly doubled. At the same time, the number of people working on farms dropped by half during these decades. By 1960 only 8 percent of America's population was still working the land.

The smaller number of farms and farmers more than met the needs of the country's increasingly urbanized society. In the 1950s agricultural abundance had become a visible symbol of America's prosperity. Whereas the typical European family spent about a third of its household budget on food—and the Russian family about half—the average American family spent only a fifth of its budget on food. Rural America itself showed the signs of a rising standard of living; cars, televisions, and electrical appliances became increasingly commonplace. The upward trend in income, however, favored the owners of large operations over smaller farms.

Changing Times on the Farm Front

The new agricultural revolution created problems of transition for the American farmer. Investment in new machinery, chemicals, and seed was expensive. Although farmers could cover more ground, they also needed much more land in order to compete. They needed to produce more to be profitable, yet overproduction forced prices down and cut into profits. Despite more efficiency, making ends meet became increasingly difficult, especially for the small farmer.

During the 1930s the federal government tried to solve the problem of overproduction by paying farmers not to plant certain crops and by **subsidizing** market prices. The government also began buying and storing the extra food that farmers produced. Although these policies helped many farmers stay afloat during the Depression, over the next decades the government's efforts did little to reduce the pressures that were squeezing out small farmers. Large-scale operations benefited the most from crop-control programs and other government aid. Many small farms either failed or sold out to larger farms. Rural Americans continued to move in droves to urban areas.

Modern farming was becoming increasingly specialized. Large-scale farmers depended more and more on chemicals to restore soil, control pests, and promote quick growth. In the 1950s there was not yet a deep concern about the overuse of chemicals in agriculture. Little was known about their effect on animals, humans, and the earth.

SCIENCE AND TECHNOLOGY

"One of the most important concepts of twentieth-century invention," wrote historian Frederick Lewis Allen in 1950, was "the idea that man could produce materials . . . superior to what nature could produce." In 1955 philosopher Morris Ernst predicted control over the weather by 1976. "Man will be master. Weather will be his servant," he wrote. In 1959 Las Vegas celebrated "cleaner bomb testing" with the crowning of "Miss Atomic Blast."

In the postwar era, many Americans were flush with the belief that science could do anything and that miraculous technological advances would continue to change life for the better. They believed that science and technology could and would eventually solve all of the world's toughest problems.

AT A GLANCE

▶ The Atomic Age

▶ Technology Changes the Way People Live and Work

▶ A New Frontier

▶ The Discovery of DNA

▶ The Miracle Workers

▶ Silent Spring

World War II had given a big boost to scientific and technological developments. After the war, the government continued to finance research, and major advances continued at a rate never before achieved. Public health care improved because of new knowledge and new medicines. People also enjoyed the benefits of science and technology in their everyday lives, in the form of new labor-saving devices, faster services, and new means of entertainment.

Yet evidence was all around that the blessings of scientific progress were mixed at best. A powerful symbol of this was the atomic bomb (above). Born of research and discovery about the invisible structure of the universe, the bomb was evidence of what havoc human designs could wreak on nature.

DATAFILE

Science

Life expectancy at birth (yrs.)	1946	1963
Males	64.4	66.6
Females	69.4	73.4

Top five causes of death, 1946–1963

1. Heart and kidney diseases   2. Cancer
3. Influenza and pneumonia   4. Accidents (not involving motor vehicles)   5. Motor vehicle accidents

Technology

Miles of paved roads

1946 .... 1.7 mil.   1963 .... 2.7 mil.

Passenger miles traveled, 1963

Rail .... 18.5 bil.   Air .... 50.4 bil.

Households in 1963 with . . .

Electricity	100%
Telephone	81%
Indoor plumbing	82%

THE SPACE RACE BEGINS
Federal Government Expenditures on Space Research and Technology, 1946–1963

Source: U.S. Office of Management and Budget.

THE ATOMIC AGE

When the first atomic bombs were used at Hiroshima and Nagasaki in 1945, the world was shocked at their awesome power. To jubilant Americans at the end of the war, the future importance of these far-off blasts was not yet clear. Over the next year, as America's attention shifted toward the Cold War, the dilemmas of the new atomic age began to be felt. Though there were obvious dangers in the continued development of nuclear weapons, many people saw a greater danger in not having weapons superior to those of the Soviet Union. Atomic research also opened new frontiers of science and offered new sources of energy; at the same time, it created the capability for destroying the planet.

The atomic bomb came about from intensive wartime research. In late 1939 President Roosevelt learned that the Germans might be working on a weapon that would use the power of **nuclear fission**—atom splitting. Concerned, he asked American scientists to pool their research and develop a similar weapon quickly. In 1942, under tight Army control, American scientists and engineers began a highly secret atomic weapons program called the "Manhattan Project." By 1945, the team at Los Alamos, New Mexico, had built two fission bombs. The power of these weapons was demonstrated on the two Japanese cities.

After the war, the United States continued development of atomic bombs. In 1946 it conducted its first peacetime test near Bikini Island in the Pacific, and several other tests followed there. Although America's nuclear technology was a closely guarded secret, the United States lost its monopoly in atomic weapons in 1949, when the Soviet Union set off its first fission bomb. After that, President Truman ordered scientists to speed up work on a new kind of weapon—one that employed the vast potential energy of nuclear fusion (a merging together of atoms). This fusion device, called a "hydrogen bomb," would have many times the destructive capability of an A-bomb. The United States tested the first H-bomb at Eniwetok, a coral island in the Pacific, in November 1952. A fireball six times hotter than the sun turned the mile-long island into a crater. Less than a year later, the Soviets exploded a similar device in Siberia.

Perils and Promise

Exploding nuclear bombs created **fallout**—both physical and political. Before Hiroshima and Nagasaki, the long-term effects of an atomic blast—widespread contamination, radiation sickness, and cancer—were relatively unknown. As these effects became realized, the fear of mass destruction became tinged with a vision of a world made uninhabitable. The testing of ever larger and more powerful weapons gave people more to fear. In 1954 the United States destroyed Bikini with the largest bomb it ever tested, a 15-megaton H-bomb named *Bravo.* It was 750 times more powerful than the A-bomb that destroyed Hiroshima.

After the *Bravo* blast, which sent radioactive ash raining over a wide area of the Pacific, people around the world became more concerned about the dangers of nuclear testing in the atmosphere. In 1958 the United States, the USSR, and Great Britain (which had tested its first A-bomb in 1952) temporarily agreed to conduct tests underground. In 1963 these nuclear powers signed a test-ban treaty that outlawed nuclear tests in the atmosphere.

Some people questioned any kind of testing of nuclear bombs. Citizens' groups such as SANE, the Committee for a Sane Nuclear Policy, urged people to support a less-intensive nuclear policy. Even J. Robert Oppenheimer, the man who

Living with the Bomb

As the shock wave of the atomic age spread across the United States in the 1950s, it prompted many different reactions. The possibility of nuclear war made people consider how they would protect themselves in an attack. Some people prepared for the worst. As the Cold War intensified, they expected the Russians to attack at any moment.

The government prepared programs for civil defense, or the protection of civilians during war. In classrooms across the country, children practiced "duck and cover" drills, throwing themselves under their desks at the sound of a civil defense siren. They also learned where to find government-built fallout shelters.

Some families went so far as to build bomb shelters in their basements or backyards. Newspapers and government pamphlets provided the plans and listed essential supplies, such as canned food and water, blankets, and a radio. A few companies took advantage of the fad by selling ready-made and ready-supplied shelters, complete with radiation detectors and protective suits.

had directed the creation of the first atom bombs, doubted the wisdom of nuclear buildup. Oppenheimer opposed development of the potentially catastrophic H-bomb. His stand drew criticism from those who supported a strong nuclear defense program, and hard-liners accused him of communist sympathies. In 1954 he was prevented from doing any further consulting for the government's nuclear program.

Recognizing the potential of atomic energy for peacetime use, scientists looked for other applications. The Atomic Energy Commission was established in 1946 to set safety rules and control all facilities, research, and information related to atomic energy. Under President Eisenhower, "Atoms for Peace" was established in 1953, and the Atomic Energy Act of 1954 authorized private companies to own and operate nuclear power plants. In 1957 the first nuclear-powered plant to produce electricity for public use began operation outside of Pittsburgh, Pennsylvania. Several years earlier, the U.S. Navy had launched the first nuclear-powered submarine, the U.S.S. *Nautilus.*

▲ After World War II, J. Robert Oppenheimer became an adviser to the U.S. Atomic Energy Commission, the agency that replaced the Manhattan Project. He helped shape U.S. policy on nuclear weapons and energy in the postwar years, but he became increasingly concerned about the bomb he had helped create.

Technology

TECHNOLOGY CHANGES THE WAY PEOPLE LIVE AND WORK

Aided by discoveries in physics and chemistry, technology took enormous steps after World War II. In 1948 two physicists at Bell Lab-oratories, Walter Brattain and John Bardeen, invented the first transistor. Experimenting with semiconductors—solids that sometimes act like conductors and sometimes do not—they developed a device that acts like a little electronic switch, controlling the flow of electrical current between two points. Three years later their co-worker, William Shockley, invented another type of transistor using the semiconductor silicon. Most modern transistors are based on his device. As a result of their work, all three scientists won the Nobel Prize for physics in 1956.

The transistor became one of the great inventions in the history of electronics. These tiny, efficient, and durable components eventually replaced vacuum tubes in radios and televisions (early transistors were only 1/200th the size of the bulky vacuum tube). Transistors made possible such products as portable radios and televisions, minicalculators, and integrated circuits for computer memory.

COMPUTER BUG

To computer users today, a "bug" is a flaw or error in a computer program. This usage came about in 1945 when a dead moth was found trapped in the electrical parts of the Mark I, one of the first computers, causing it to fail.

"Necessity," the saying goes, "is the mother of invention." But during and after World War II, the Cold War and then U.S.-Soviet competition in outer space drove the development of most advanced technologies.

Government and industry backed research projects far too expensive and complex to be pushed forward by individual inventors. With vast financial resources, the government and large corporations could attract and organize well-trained problem-solvers. They were put to work in groups called "think tanks" to advance weapons, space, and other complex technologies. The government gave billions of dollars in grants to fund private research facilities such as Bell Labs and the Rand Corporation.

In universities across the country, the emphasis also turned to science and technology. Almost a third of all university researchers were involved in weapons research. By 1959 the federal government was budgeting $5.3 billion for missile development alone.

The Computer Revolution

Like many other technological advances, computers grew out of the military's need for faster and more accurate machines during World War II. In 1942 scientists at the University of Pennsylvania began building an electronic computer to carry out the complex calculations necessary for aiming missiles. Unveiled in 1946, this machine was called ENIAC (Electrical Numerical Integrator and Calculator). ENIAC was huge, expensive, and difficult to operate—it had to be rewired for each new task. But it was the beginning of the age of the digital computer.

Progress came quickly in the years following the war. American mathematician John von Neumann suggested in 1946 that computers use stored programs rather than rely on rewiring. Modern programmable electronic computers began appearing in the late 1940s. They generally employed random access memory (RAM), which gave easier access to any particular piece of information. The develop-

ments of magnetic recording tape and transistors allowed ever more sophisticated computers to be developed during the 1950s. The new machines were still huge and very expensive to purchase and operate. They were generally found only in large computer centers shared by industry, government, and private laboratories.

Large businesses quickly found applications for these miracle machines. As time went on and as more people learned how to operate computers, the machines became more common. Computers sped up business office operations and made them more accurate. They also helped in manufacturing processes by doing repetitive, assembly-line tasks.

Computers had some drawbacks, though. When automation took jobs away from workers, computers got blamed. When people got aggravated with too much paperwork, excessive "red tape," lost data, or calculation errors, they pointed fingers at the computer. Also, at first people dreaded

► Filling a whole room, ENIAC contained 18,000 vacuum tubes and weighed 30 tons. ENIAC's inventors (foreground, center), John W. Mauchly and J. Presper Eckert Jr., went on to build UNIVAC I, the first commercially available computer.

the huge size of computers and the difficulty of operating them. Computer centers had to be staffed with many programmers and specially trained support personnel.

The Power of Light

Albert Einstein and others had realized the basic principles of the laser long before the first one was successfully demonstrated. In 1953 a device that produced a concentrated beam of radio waves—the maser (which stands for microwave amplification by stimulated emission of radiation)—was invented. The principle of the maser led to the development of the optical maser, or laser (light amplification by stimulated emission of radiation), in 1960 by American physicist Theodore Maiman.

A laser emits an intense, concentrated beam of light that moves in one direction. All portions of the light wave vibrate together, unlike ordinary light sources that emit light of different frequencies. A laser beam can be sent over large distances without spreading out like ordinary light. It can also be focused to a very small spot with very high intensity.

Researchers developed many kinds of lasers in the early 1960s, and they discovered many uses for laser technology. New uses are being found every day. Doctors routinely perform certain kinds of surgery, particularly eye surgery, with lasers. The high power of lasers makes them useful to industry for welding, cutting, and drilling. They also have countless applications for scientific research. Because lasers can carry thousands of messages at once, they

Grace Hopper: Computer Pioneer

▲ As a Navy lieutenant during World War II, Hopper worked on the computing machines that came before electronic computers.

Grace Murray Hopper was born in New York City on December 9, 1906. She received a Ph.D. in mathematics from Yale University. During World War II, she was instrumental in developing computation methods for the U.S. Navy. After the war she joined the U.S. Naval Reserves and worked on the UNIVAC computer project for private industry.

In the early 1950s, Hopper became widely known in scientific circles for her pioneering work designing compilers for the computer industry. A compiler is a type of computer software that can translate high-level computer languages into elementary machine language so that a particular computer is able to use it.

Hopper also helped develop the Common Business Oriented Language (COBOL). It was one of the first high-level computer languages. A high-level computer language is flexible and natural, similar to ordinary human language. COBOL is used mainly to do business tasks such as billing and payroll.

Grace Hopper retired from the Navy in 1986 as a rear admiral and died in January 1992.

"The schools are in terrible shape. . . . What has long been an ignored material problem, Sputnik has made a recognized crisis. . . . [The] spartan Soviet system is producing many students better equipped to cope with the technicalities of the Space Age."

—*Life* editorial, 1958

▶ The launch of *Sputnik 1* on October 5, 1957, began the space age. Carrying a radio transmitter and a thermometer, the aluminum orb was 23 inches in diameter and weighed 184 pounds. Scientists and radio operators around the world reported picking up its beeping radio signal during its three months in orbit.

are becoming increasingly important for long-distance communications. Lasers made possible the technology for compact disks, a recording medium that digitally stores audio, video, or text information. Lasers will eventually be used in computer microprocessing, which will permit computers to operate hundreds of times faster.

Space

A NEW FRONTIER

In 1957 and 1958 three Soviet space satellites named *Sputnik* ("traveling companion") caught the United States completely off guard. This show of Soviet superiority in rocket science shook America's self-confidence. Americans already worried about the "missile gap" could not imagine what had gone

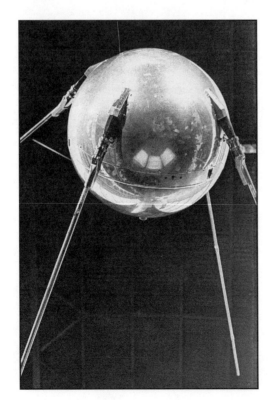

wrong. To set things right, the government poured huge sums of money into science education, which had already been strengthened because of the Cold War. The *Sputnik* satellites sparked the beginning of the "space race" between the United States and the Soviet Union.

The *Sputnik*s' scientific purpose was mainly to investigate outer space and to discover if living organisms could survive its conditions. *Sputnik 2*, launched on November 3, 1957, carried Laika, a small dog, with equipment for recording her pulse, respiration, blood pressure, and heartbeat. She was kept alive for ten days and proved that living creatures could survive weightlessness and other unknown conditions of space. Laika's craft was not designed to return her to Earth.

The Space Race Gets off the Ground

In the United States, the Army and Navy had competed over which one would launch into orbit the first American satellite. In 1955 the Navy's Project Vanguard was chosen, but many administrative and technical problems delayed the program. After the first two *Sputnik*s, the Army pushed ahead its own program. The first U.S. satellite, the missile-shaped *Explorer 1*, left Cape Canaveral, Florida, atop an Army Jupiter C rocket on January 31, 1958. The objective of the first and later *Explorer*s was to investigate the earth's shape, surface, and levels of atmosphere. They also explored space among the planets and certain phenomena concerning stars. Among *Ex-*

plorer 1's major contributions was its discovery of the Van Allen radiation belts surrounding the earth. These are belts of intense radiation that circle the earth in the outer atmosphere.

It was soon clear that to avoid competition between the armed services, the United States needed a single agency to conduct nonmilitary space research. In 1958 Congress created NASA, the National Aeronautics and Space Administration. Teams of scientists and engineers continued to develop rockets and satellites, exploring ways to put a human in space.

For the next several years, NASA seemed to be playing catch-up with its Soviet counterpart. NASA rushed forward with Project Mercury, the initial phase of its piloted space program, but the Soviets were the first to send a human into space. On April 12, 1961, cosmonaut Yury Gagarin was launched out of the atmosphere in the *Vostok 1* spacecraft. He circled the earth once.

Less than a month later, on May 5, astronaut Alan Shepard became the first American launched into space. Almost a year later, John Glenn became the first American to orbit the earth. Glenn's nearly five-hour flight took him around the globe three times. By this time, the United States and USSR were evenly matched in the space race.

President John F. Kennedy recognized the degree to which America's imagination was captured by the wonders of the space age. In an address to the nation in 1962, he promised that the nation would land a man on the moon by the end

Mercury Missions

Crew	Orbits	Duration	Date
Alan B. Shepard Jr.	0	15 min., 22 sec.	May 5, 1961
Virgil I. Grissom	0	15 min., 37 sec.	July 21, 1961
John H. Glenn Jr.	3	4 hrs., 55 min., 23 sec.	February 20, 1962
M. Scott Carpenter	3	4 hrs., 56 min., 05 sec.	May 24, 1962
Walter M. Schirra Jr.	6	9 hrs., 13 min., 11 sec.	October 3, 1962
L. Gordon Cooper	22	34 hrs., 19 min., 49 sec.	May 15 and 16, 1963

The first seven U.S. astronauts (above, from left: Schirra, Shepard, Grissom, Donald K. Slayton, Glenn, Carpenter, and Cooper) were test pilots recruited in 1959 from the armed services. All but Slayton flew in Mercury missions. Glenn (right) traveled in the capsule *Friendship 7* in his historic orbital flight.

The Mercury astronauts underwent intensive physical and psychological tests and training to prepare for the unknown rigors of solo space flight. Nobody knew for sure that humans could endure the forces of lift-off and reentry and the weightlessness of space. And the astronauts' survival was almost completely dependent on new technology. Facing these unknowns demanded enormous courage.

Yeager Wins Race with Sound

In June 1948 the U.S. Army announced that eight months earlier, Air Force major Charles Yeager had flown his supersonic aircraft, a Bell X-1, faster than the speed of sound. The plane reached a speed of 967 miles per hour, breaking the sound barrier for the first time.

of the 1960s. In 1969 America established its lead when astronaut Neil Armstrong landed on the moon.

The space programs of the United States and USSR would never have gotten off the ground without numerous other scientific and technological developments, including computers and the miniaturized electronics made possible by transistors. In the United States, materials and technologies designed for the space program had many applications in business and industry, including commercial aviation and communications. The American satellite *Telstar 1*, launched from Cape Canaveral on July 10, 1962, transmitted the first direct television pictures from the United States to Europe.

Science

THE DISCOVERY OF DNA

In early 1953 a 24-year-old American, James Watson, wrote about "a strange model" with several unusual features that he and a British scientist, Francis Crick, were building. In April they unveiled this model, which presented the molecular structure of a substance called deoxyribonucleic acid, or DNA. DNA is a complex molecule carrying hereditary information that directs the growth of every cell. The model that Watson and Crick built depicted DNA's "double helix" formation (*helix* means "spiral"), so called because the molecules form twin coils, chained together like a winding staircase. Today, their breakthrough in the understanding of **genetics** is considered one of the most significant of all time.

The modern study of genetics had begun in 1865, when Austrian monk Gregor Mendel demonstrated the inheritance patterns of the garden pea. His theories were based on hereditary factors, or what we now call genes. Mendel knew that something like genes must exist, although he did not know what exactly carried the hereditary information.

Although the substance of DNA was first detected in the early twentieth century, it was not until the mid-1940s that biologists began to determine how it might function. By the early 1950s, scientists studying certain bacteria had confirmed that genes were made up of DNA. In 1951 two acquaintances of Watson and Crick, British scientists Maurice Wilkins and Rosalind Franklin, used special X-ray techniques to discover how the DNA molecule looked. Their X-ray pictures suggested that the overall shape was a double helix.

That same year, the young zoologist Watson met the physicist-turned-biologist Crick, and the two set about to determine the exact makeup of the DNA molecule based on the X-ray work of Wilkins and Franklin. They determined that the steps of the DNA ladder were made up of pairs of special chemicals. The pattern of these chemical steps determined the unique quality of the genetic makeup of every living thing. Furthermore, the DNA molecule re-created itself by splitting down the middle of the staircase—like a zipper unzipping—and each half re-formed its missing parts.

The Watson-Crick model was a major step in genetic research because it answered many questions about how DNA functions and multiplies. For these discoveries, Watson and Crick shared the 1962 Nobel Prize for medicine with Wilkins. This model of the basic "building blocks" of life had a great impact on the biological sciences, opening new avenues of research in genetics, biochemistry, and medicine.

Medicine

THE MIRACLE WORKERS

It is now hard to imagine a world in which children commonly died from measles, scarlet fever, tuberculosis, and polio. Yet, before the medical breakthroughs that began with World War II, that was the case. After the war, modern medicine took major steps toward treating common illnesses, particularly childhood diseases, with new vaccines and "wonder drugs." The average American's life span increased significantly.

In 1952 Jonas Salk developed the first effective vaccine against poliomyelitis (or polio), a crippling, often fatal disease. Polio was also called "infantile paralysis" because it struck mainly children. Used experimentally during a 1953 polio **epidemic,** the vaccine (made of dead polio viruses) came into widespread use by 1955. In 1960 Albert Sabin introduced a live virus vaccine that could be taken orally. It soon replaced the Salk vaccine because it was cheaper, easier to use and store, and longer lasting. Both vaccines helped make the dreaded disease a rarity in the United States.

New medicines revolutionized medical care, starting with the

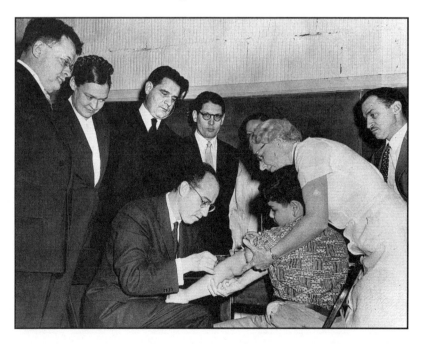

▼ Dr. Jonas Salk administers his polio vaccine to a Pittsburgh boy in 1956. A team of Soviet doctors visiting the United States watches the immunization take place.

Dr. Spock: Child Care Revolutionary

▲ Dr. Spock (center) dispenses advice to mothers and their children.

Dr. Benjamin Spock is famous both for his theories on child care and for his leadership in the peace movement. His best-selling 1946 book, *The Common Sense Book of Baby and Child Care*, changed the way parents thought about raising their children.

Earlier child care books had favored rigid feeding and bedtime schedules. They also claimed that it was harmful to show children too much affection. Spock's book sought to reassure mothers by supporting their naturally arising feelings of maternal tenderness.

Spock also answered practical questions not even addressed by earlier works. Mothers today still consult the book about concerns such as teething, toilet training, and bed-wetting. Even though Spock was later accused of encouraging "permissiveness" in his book, he actually suggested that parents set standards and expectations for their children.

Spock showed no political interest until President John F. Kennedy announced in 1962 that the United States would resume nuclear testing to stay ahead of the Soviet Union. Deeply concerned, Spock predicted a nuclear accident or war. He warned about the dangers of nuclear fallout to children especially—by such means as the radioactive contamination of milk, for example. During the Vietnam War, Spock led peace marches. He ran for president in 1972 as a candidate of the People's party.

antibiotic penicillin. First used to treat the wounded of World War II, penicillin came into common use after the war. Its success prompted a search for other such drugs, and several more were soon discovered. Antibiotics were found to cure a variety of common infectious diseases, such as tonsillitis, tuberculosis, and pneumonia.

Other types of drugs were soon developed. The hormone cortisone was first used in 1948 to relieve arthritis symptoms. Cortisone was also found to relieve inflammations from poison ivy and various skin diseases and has been used to treat leukemia, especially in children. Another useful class of drug, antihistamines, was developed in 1950 and used to treat all sorts of allergy symptoms. Finally, in the mid-1950s, tranquilizers first came into use. They began to change completely the treatment of many mentally ill patients.

Another major step in this era was the development of many synthetic drugs by chemists in the laboratory. High technology also made innovative surgical techniques possible. Open-heart surgery was pioneered during this era. Doctors also first performed certain transplant operations, including the replacement of weakened arteries with plastic tubes.

Lifestyle Changes

The era of modern medicine created new choices and concerns. The baby boom focused medical attention on the proper care of women during pregnancy and of their children after birth. The baby-boom era also produced the first birth-control pill. Developed as a result of hormone reseach in the mid-1950s, "the Pill" came into wide use in the 1960s.

As new information about nutrition became available, people became more aware of the importance of eating properly. Many prepared foods became fortified with added vitamins. Other additives, such as preservatives, were put into food as well. These kept foods from spoiling, but some were later found to be harmful.

In 1953 scientists established the link between cigarette smoking and lung cancer. Four years later the surgeon general issued an official warning about the effect smoking had on health. This marked the beginning of a growing appreciation in the medical community of the importance of prevention in combating diseases.

Overall, middle-class prosperity meant that people could afford better health care and that it was more widely available. Not everyone benefited from the new medical breakthroughs, however. The ongoing cycle of poverty in the lower classes, particularly among underprivileged minorities, kept some people from getting the medical care they needed.

Environment

SILENT SPRING

In the 1950s the rapid growth of industry, technology, and population gave people a tremendous sense of pride in themselves and in the "American way." Families had nicer homes, bigger and better cars, more money to spend, more things to buy, and more children to buy things for. What could possibly go wrong in this best of all possible worlds?

Then, in 1962, Rachel Carson's *Silent Spring* appeared, first as a series of articles for *The New Yorker* magazine, and then as a book. Carson, whose two previous best-sellers had been about the ocean, turned to the earth and the life that inhabits it. *Silent Spring* called attention to the dangers of herbicides and pesticides, which she called "biocides," because she felt they could potentially kill all life. Carson's main target was DDT, an insecticide that had been widely used during and after World War II to combat malaria, a disease carried by mosquitoes. She blamed DDT for the endangerment or disappearance of many species of birds.

The chemical industry fiercely attacked her book, questioning its scientific basis. Eventually, however, public reaction to the book led to the banning of DDT and stimulated other environmental protection measures. Later research proved that DDT builds up in the food chain and concentrates in the systems of larger organisms, perhaps even humans. Some birds, such as falcons and eagles, showed the effects of DDT by laying eggs that were deformed or infertile. *Silent Spring* helped trigger a new environmental movement. It made people think about things they had not really wanted to face before. What are the side effects of all this technology? And can we really enjoy all this progress without paying a stiff environmental price?

ARTS AND ENTERTAINMENT

In the 1950s Americans pursued leisure with enthusiasm. They painted by number, played board games, hunted and fished, listened to music, and read Reader's Digest condensed books. But more than anything, they watched television.

Owning a television set meant status, entertainment, and comfort. Television helped people forget their fears about the Cold War and the Bomb. It brought families together in their cozy suburban living rooms. A television culture began to develop. That culture was informed by TV Guide (founded in 1952), and its members were fed by frozen TV dinners (introduced in 1954). Television became a new kind of baby-sitter for a generation of Baby Boomers. By 1956 Americans spent 42

AT A GLANCE

▶ **Television's Golden Age**

▶ **Hollywood Heads Downhill**

▶ **The Sound of Music**

▶ **Rock Around the Clock**

▶ **The Culture of Conformity**

▶ **The Arts Go Abstract**

hours a week watching television—more time than they spent at work.

Americans believed that television was bringing them all together—a nation of wholesome, middle-class consumers. Once the payments were made, TV was free and available to everyone. It could focus on anything, anywhere, live. It was more than mass entertainment—it was a window to the world.

At the end of the era Americans were indeed brought together by television. Millions experienced the horror of President Kennedy's assassination. They saw his alleged murderer shot before their eyes. They wept at the funeral. The world had changed—people knew it was true because they saw it on television.

DATAFILE

Attendance and sales	1946	1963
Movie attendance (weekly)	90 mil.	42 mil.
Reading material sales (excluding educational)	$1.7 bil.	$4.1 bil.
Home audio/visual expenditures	$1.2 bil.	$5.4 bil.

The press	1946	1963
Number of daily newspapers	1,763	1,754
Circulation	50.9 mil.	58.9 mil.

	1947	1958
Number of magazines	4,610	4,455
Circulation	384.6 mil.	408.4 mil.

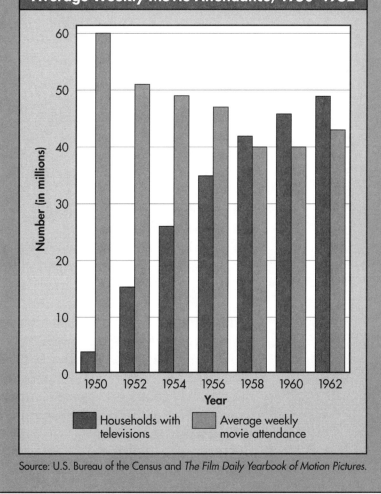

TELEVISION'S IMPACT ON THE MOVIE INDUSTRY
Households with Televisions, Average Weekly Movie Attendance, 1950–1962

Legend: Households with televisions; Average weekly movie attendance

Source: U.S. Bureau of the Census and *The Film Daily Yearbook of Motion Pictures.*

TELEVISION'S GOLDEN AGE

Watching television became the most popular form of entertainment in the 1950s. The booming postwar consumer market and the newness of television created a huge demand for sets. By the end of the fifties 87 percent of all American families owned at least one set. Homemakers watched soap operas while they ironed. Kids watched old movies when they got home from school. Their parents watched the evening news while they looked over the daily newspaper. Families watched "prime time" shows after dinner. From cities to suburbs to small towns and farms, Americans tuned in to the same television programs and events—they shared the same entertainment and experiences.

The Early Days

Television did not really become popular until the late 1940s. Some TV broadcasts of news and sporting events were aired early in the decade, but World War II slowed the development of television. After the war network broadcasting quickly resumed and expanded, and local TV stations arose all across the country.

Soon everybody was buying TV sets. In 1946 only 8,000 families owned a set. By 1950 nearly 4 million families had at least one set. By the early 1960s that figure was close to 50 million families.

From the late 1940s to the late 1950s, most television programs were broadcast live. Many of the earliest shows were based on older

Today, almost all television broadcasts are in color. Until 1953, however, all programs had been telecast in black and white. Color television really took off in 1954, when the Radio Corporation of America (RCA) began producing color sets. They sold for about $1,000. Fourteen years later—and at a much lower price—color sets outsold black-and-white sets for the first time.

kinds of entertainment. Popular variety shows, such as those hosted by Milton Berle, Ed Sullivan, and Jackie Gleason, came from the vaudeville tradition. The host introduced a variety of guests who sang, danced, did stand-up comedy, or juggled. Many performers—some who later became stars—were introduced to the American public for the first time on these shows. For example, Sid Caesar's *Your Show of Shows* spawned a whole generation of comedians and comedy writers, such as Carl Reiner, Mel Brooks, and Woody Allen.

Television also adapted radio comedy, soap operas, and drama series, such as *Dragnet* and *The Lone Ranger*. Radio stars moved to television along with their shows. The switch could either make or break them, depending on how they looked on the screen. Some talented performers—like Lucille Ball—had been in show business for some years, but now their careers took off.

Television also made a point of developing programs to reach the growing number of children. The Baby Boom created a vast market of consumers that advertisers yearned to reach. Networks responded with *The Howdy Doody Show, Captain Kangaroo, The Mickey Mouse Club*, and Saturday-morning cartoons.

People still refer to the 1950s as television's "Golden Age." The new industry was exciting, and it showed a variety of programs. Early forms of the programming common today began to emerge. There were family-oriented situation comedies, like *I Love Lucy, Leave It to Beaver*, and *Father Knows Best*. There were action series like *The Untouchables, Hawaiian Eye*, and *Gunsmoke*. There were the game shows *Queen for a Day, Truth or Consequences*, and *Beat the Clock* and the panel show *What's My Line?* Another early creation was the television special or "spectacular," which filled an evening with a one-time-only dramatic, musical, or variety event.

Live Drama in the Living Room

Live drama had an important place on television in the early 1950s. In those days, Hollywood movie studios would not allow their feature films to be shown on television, so the New York–based networks created their own drama instead. They turned to Broadway performers and directors and commissioned original plays from serious writers. Several regular shows—*Philco TV Playhouse, Kraft Television Theatre, The U.S. Steel Hour*, and *Playhouse 90*—presented high-quality

▼ Lucille Ball (left) as Lucy Ricardo and Vivian Vance as Ethel Mertz play to two audiences—in the studio and in homes across the country—in a scene from *I Love Lucy*.

plays. Actors such as Paul Newman began their moves to stardom in these dramas.

These dramatic productions got high ratings, but they were expensive and difficult to produce. They were also risky. Because they were live, millions of viewers would see any mistakes. They could not be rerun either, which cut down on profits. Advertisers disliked their serious tone. Instead, they preferred light-hearted situation comedies or variety shows. They were safer and easier to sell.

Classical music was also broadcast live on television. For example, Arturo Toscanini's NBC Orchestra began playing on television as well as on radio. In 1948 audiences saw and heard Gian Carlo Menotti's two short operatic works, *The Medium* and *The Telephone* live from Philadelphia. These concerts and operas, too, were expensive to produce.

Networks and Advertising

The television airwaves were full of another sound—commercials. Sales of Kraft cheese rose significantly because of the company's advertising on *Kraft Television Theatre*. This demonstrated how powerful television's sales potential could be. The advertising techniques perfected in radio were now turned toward television with an added element—pictures. Catchy jingles were aided by images. New characters, like "Speedy" Alka-Seltzer, began to promote products. People enjoyed the ads and considered them another type of entertainment.

Revenue from ads, of course, fueled the network system. From the beginning, three major radio networks, CBS, NBC, and ABC, had dominated the TV industry. Most local stations had an arrangement with one of the major networks, and these networks created much of the programming seen across the country. Smaller networks existed, but they found it difficult to compete with the nationally broadcast programs of the majors. By 1955 only the big three networks were left. One reason smaller networks suffered: the wider a show was broadcast, the more viewers it had—and the more desirable it was to advertisers.

The relation of the networks and major advertisers became the subject of controversy in the late 1950s. Network quiz shows, such as *Twenty-One* and *The $64,000 Question*, drew large, faithful audiences. These audiences attracted sponsors, who wanted to get their products seen by as many people as possible. However, in 1958, a *Twenty-One* contestant revealed that these shows were usually rigged. Certain contestants—depending on how popular they were

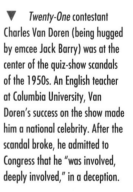

▼ *Twenty-One* contestant Charles Van Doren (being hugged by emcee Jack Barry) was at the center of the quiz-show scandals of the 1950s. An English teacher at Columbia University, Van Doren's success on the show made him a national celebrity. After the scandal broke, he admitted to Congress that he "was involved, deeply involved," in a deception.

BIRTHS . . .

Cher, singer-actress, 1946
Mikhail Baryshnikov, dancer, 1948
Garry Trudeau, cartoonist, 1948
Roseanne Barr Arnold, comedienne, 1952
Eddie Murphy, comedian, 1961

. . . AND DEATHS

W. C. Fields, comedian, 1946
Humphrey Bogart, actor, 1957
Arturo Toscanini, conductor, 1957
Lou Costello, comedian, 1959
Clark Gable, actor, 1960

with audiences—were fed the answers to questions ahead of time. Viewers were shocked, and congressional hearings looked into the scandal. The American public learned how tight a control sponsors and networks had on television programming and how far they would go to increase the "entertainment value" of their shows. Afterward, the networks tried to improve their image by offering more public affairs programs.

Covering the News

Television has always demonstrated an extraordinary ability to cover important events. It aired Senator Estes Kefauver's investigations into organized crime in 1950–1951 and Joe McCarthy's sensational Army hearings in 1954. Television also added a new dimension to political campaigning. Dwight D. Eisenhower's strategy of spot commercials and short speeches worked well in his 1952 presidential campaign. On the other hand, Adlai E. Stevenson's longer speeches were less effective and harder for viewers to understand. By the 1960 presidential campaign, nine of ten homes had television sets, and many people used television as a major source of political information. Nearly 80 percent of the voters saw at least one of the 1960 debates between candidates John F. Kennedy and Richard M. Nixon.

Although radio had been effective in reporting news events instantly, it was not as influential as television became. Television affected newspapers and magazines even more than it did radio. Because people could see events actually happening, printed news stories and photographs became less appealing. Mass-circulation general magazines began to lose readers, marking the beginning of the end for weekly magazines such as *Life* and *Look.* On the other hand, special-interest publications like *Sports Illustrated* became very popular.

Impact on Culture

In 1961 the head of the Federal Communications Commission (FCC), Newton Minow, described television as a "vast wasteland" of "game shows, violence, sadism, murder, western badmen, western goodmen, private eyes, gangsters, more violence, and cartoons." These criticisms were not new, however. A decade earlier Daniel Marsh, the president of Boston University, had been even more critical. "If the television craze continues with the present level of programs," he warned, "we are destined to have a nation of morons."

For better or worse, the "idiot box" or "boob tube" did change people's lives. Living-room furniture was moved to face the set. Some of the mass-produced homes in Levittown on Long Island had sets built into the walls. People bought TV trays, TV dinners, and *TV Guide.* The mass appeal of television and advertising raised expectations for a higher standard of living. And the mass reach of the medium ended a sense of remoteness and isolation for many in society.

People throughout the world debated television's impact. Did it provide a distorted view of the world? Did it really bring the family together, or did family members merely sit in the same room without communicating? Critics discussed television's impact on America's youth. A national survey showed that children watched 27 hours of television each week, just 45 minutes less than the time they spent in school. People today still debate what television could and should be, but the tube plays on.

The Hollywood Ten: Witch Hunts in the Movies

◄ Animator Walt Disney, shown taking an oath before HUAC, testified that communists once "took over" his artists but that his studios had since employed "100 percent Americans."

The threat of communist subversion at home struck fear into the hearts of many Americans. The threat, it turned out, was largely an illusion for which the U.S. House Un-American Activities Committee (HUAC) was mainly responsible.

In the 1930s conservatives in Congress formed HUAC to expose alleged communist influence in the New Deal. In 1947 HUAC began hearings to expose communists in other segments of society. Critics called this activity "witch hunts."

Many people who believed in workers' rights and disliked **racism** had joined the Communist party in the 1930s. Among them were film directors, actors, and writers. Ten were singled out by the committee and required to appear before Congress in October 1947. The press called them the "Hollywood Ten."

Some Hollywood celebrities cooperated with HUAC. Ronald Reagan, then president of the Screen Actors Guild, was one. These people testified against the Ten. Others, including Humphrey Bogart, Lauren Bacall, Katharine Hepburn, and Gene Kelly, participated in benefits and speeches on behalf of the Ten.

The Ten pleaded the Fifth Amendment, choosing to remain silent to the questions posed by the committee. They were held in contempt of Congress for refusing to testify, and as a result, they served jail sentences of about a year each. When they were released, however, they found that they were **blacklisted** by 50 top film executives—no one would hire them. Some of the people who had supported them either had difficulty finding work or were not used in films. These conditions lasted for several years until public opinion began to change.

The controversy had another effect as well. After the hearings Hollywood produced more movies with an openly anticommunist point of view. Between 1947 and 1954 it is estimated that more than 50 films were released that portrayed communists as enemies of the United States.

Movies

HOLLYWOOD HEADS DOWNHILL

"Hollywood's like Egypt," said producer David Selznick in 1951. "Full of crumbling pyramids. It'll never come back. It'll just keep on crumbling until finally the wind blows the last studio prop across the sands."

By the early 1950s Hollywood had serious problems. In 1946 weekly attendance at movies hit a record 82 million. Just four years later weekly attendance had fallen to about 36 million. Labor troubles, higher production costs, unfavorable court rulings, and anticommunist hysteria all damaged the movie industry. Worst of all, television was luring people away from the theaters. Why travel to the theater, people thought, when you could be entertained in the comfort of your own home? Hollywood survived these challenges, but the old system of big studios did not.

▼ Filmed on location in Rome, *Ben-Hur* was typical of Hollywood's big-budget epics on classical or biblical themes. The famous chariot-race sequence took three months to film. The movie won 11 Oscars.

In the 1940s several federal court decisions forced the studios to change the way they distributed films. Then the final blow was struck. In 1948 the Supreme Court ordered film companies to give up the theater chains they owned. Producers and distributors were forced to sell each film on its individual merits. This caused film production costs to skyrocket. The system in which studios owned everything for production and distribution of films was finally dissolved in the 1950s, because it was simply too costly.

Television Takes Away Movie Audiences

"Don't be a 'Living Room Captive.' Step out and see a great movie!" invited a 1952 film-industry ad. In 1959 producer Samuel Goldwyn said, "Conditions in the industry today are worse than I have ever known them in the forty-seven years I have been connected with pictures." Television had severely cut into movie attendance.

The same factors that had made people watch more television led them to stay away from movie theaters. People had more-comfortable homes, and they wanted to spend more time with their families. Going out to the movies became less appealing to them, so they stayed home and watched television instead. Box-office receipts started dropping off in 1947, and they went steadily down until the mid-1950s. After that they leveled off—but at about half the level of the early 1940s.

To counteract the competition of television, the studios decided to make films that would bring people back to the theaters. They made big-budget, blockbuster films like *Ben-Hur* and *The Ten Commandments,* with casts of thousands. Film companies also played it safe by adapting successful Broadway musicals, such as *Oklahoma!* and *South Pacific.* These musicals and spectacles offered what television could not: color, big screens, extravagant sets, and elaborate productions. Film companies used new technologies such as the widescreen format Cinemascope and special effects such as 3-D to add interest and excitement.

Studios started spending more money on production. By 1953 million-dollar budgets for films were common. Despite all of these efforts, the industry continued to lose money. On the other hand, a small number of movies began earning money as never before. In 1953 to 1954 alone, the number of films that grossed more than $5 million was one-third as many as had done so in all previous years of movie history.

As television production moved to the West Coast, Hollywood began adjusting itself to the idea of television as inevitable. The studios started producing TV shows, and they began selling old movies to TV stations in the mid-1950s. Hollywood also found a new market for films in Baby Boomers who had become teenagers.

Hollywood and Beyond

Postwar movies reflected America's greatest hopes and worst fears. Westerns and epics featured strong and self-sacrificing heroes. James Dean and Marlon Brando played rebels without a cause. Alfred

At the Drive-In: Teens on the Move

▲ Though drive-in theaters drew adults and families, they were especially popular with the high school crowd. Teenagers found a new kind of freedom there, and the back rows especially became known as the "passion pit."

In the suburbs and the small towns of America, just about everyone old enough to drive was on wheels by the 1950s. During this period many teenagers found themselves with more free time and money to spend from jobs and allowances. A *Life* magazine survey found that teenagers owned 1.5 million cars and spent $20 million on lipstick. By the end of the 1950s the average teenager had $400 a year to spend.

Mobile teenage consumers represented a new culture. Drive-in restaurants and drive-in movies popped up across the nation. Drive-ins allowed teenagers to stay in their new little universe—their cars—while they enjoyed the good life that their money could buy. Teenagers enjoyed a new power. At restaurants, they could honk their horn for a carhop to serve them food. They could flash their lights for someone to take away the car-window tray. They could escape from parental supervision while watching movies.

In 1956 a total of 42,000 drive-in theaters pulled in a quarter of the year's total box-office receipts. Big hits included *Blackboard Jungle, Rock Around the Clock, I Was a Teen-age Werewolf, The Blob,* and other low-budget films aimed to attract the teenage audience. Drive-in owners kept their young patrons happy and buying lots of hot dogs, popcorn, and candy for hours on end by showing double and triple features.

SIDNEY POITIER WINS OSCAR

On April 13, 1964, Sidney Poitier became the first black to win an Oscar for Best Actor, the top honor given by the motion-picture industry. He won the award for his performance in *Lilies of the Field* in 1963. Poitier's success paved the way for other blacks to earn starring roles in films.

BEST MOTION PICTURE OSCAR WINNERS

1946	*The Best Years of Our Lives*
1947	*Gentleman's Agreement*
1948	*Hamlet*
1949	*All the King's Men*
1950	*All About Eve*
1951	*An American in Paris*
1952	*Greatest Show on Earth*
1953	*From Here to Eternity*
1954	*On the Waterfront*
1955	*Marty*
1956	*Around the World in 80 Days*
1957	*The Bridge on the River Kwai*
1958	*Gigi*
1959	*Ben-Hur*
1960	*The Apartment*
1961	*West Side Story*
1962	*Lawrence of Arabia*
1963	*Tom Jones*

Hitchcock's suspense films hinted at evil hiding beneath everyday things. The blossoming genre of science ficton reflected the postwar engrossment in science and technology—often tinged with Cold War fears. Sci-fi films depicted alien invasions and gross atomic mutations. Japanese sci-fi films such as *Godzilla* reflected people's fears of atomic testing.

Other foreign films made their way into American theaters as well. Italian, British, French, and Japanese film industries were recovering from World War II and making a comeback. European filmmakers like Roberto Rossellini, Federico Fellini, and François Truffaut began making their influence felt by attracting American audiences to art theaters.

Although movie attendance declined and revenues from movies decreased, foreign filmmakers and independent producers were pumping new ideas into the American movie industry. Hollywood still had some life left in it.

Theater

THE SOUND OF MUSIC

"I've Done It Before and I Can Do It Again" was the ad that dramatist Oscar Hammerstein II placed in a 1942 issue of the show-business newspaper *Variety*. He had just teamed up with composer Richard Rodgers for a new production that would mark the beginning of a successful team in musical theater.

"What happened between Oscar and me," Rodgers later said, "was almost chemical. Put the right components together, and an explosion takes place." The two came up with a musical play that arrived on Broadway as *Oklahoma!* It became one of the musical theater's greatest achievements.

Oklahoma!, Carousel, and the other Rodgers and Hammerstein musicals that followed were innovative in that they used each well-crafted song to help carry the plot. The team also worked together on *The King and I, South Pacific,* and

The Sound of Music. These three shows expanded the horizons of musicals even further. They introduced controversial subjects, such as **prejudice,** in their stories, which had not been done before.

Dramatist Alan Jay Lerner and composer Frederick Loewe provided their own hits such as *Brigadoon* and *My Fair Lady.* The title of their musical *Camelot* provided the media's name for President Kennedy's administration. In 1957 *West Side Story* came to Broadway with music by Leonard Bernstein, book by Arthur Laurents, lyrics by Stephen Sondheim, and choreography by Jerome Robbins. It retold the Romeo and Juliet story in the setting of modern urban youth culture.

Postwar Drama

While new musicals were delighting Broadway audiences, postwar dramatists were experimenting with new techniques in their exploration of human life and relationships. *Waiting for Godot,* a play by Irishman Samuel Beckett, challenged audiences with its **minimalist** style and bleak outlook on life. The Romanian-born Eugène Ionesco adopted the same tone in what he called "anti-plays," in which he deliberately tried to make audiences restless or even bored.

American playwrights wrote about the myths and ideals by which Americans measured themselves in an age of prosperity and conformity. These dramatists probed with **realism** the states of mind that people hid from others and from themselves. In his *Death of a Salesman,* Arthur Miller created the tragic character Willy Lo-

man, whose self-destruction became a symbol of lost integrity. *A Streetcar Named Desire,* now considered by many to be Tennessee Williams's finest work, came to Broadway in 1947. The drama revealed the turbulent inner lives of its characters. Edward Albee's *Who's Afraid of Virginia Woolf?* shattered the myth of the happy American family when it opened in 1963. Lorraine Hansberry's *A Raisin in the Sun* depicted a black family's attempt to rise out of the slums of Chicago.

Other changes took place on American stages in the 1950s. The major showcase for new works was shifting from the big Broadway theaters to smaller New York theaters (called "off-Broadway") and regional and university stages. These less-commercial theaters could produce work by new playwrights or plays that ran counter to the mainstream. Off-Broadway had many long-running successes, such as Kurt Weill's *Threepenny Opera,* which featured the hit song "Mack the Knife." Another offbeat musical—*The Fantasticks*—began its off-Broadway run in 1960 and continued into the 1990s. Although small-town theaters were disappearing, summer stock and dinner theaters rose in popularity.

Music

ROCK AROUND THE CLOCK

In 1955 *Life* magazine ran a pictorial article about the new "mysterious teenage music craze." "Some American parents," *Life* wrote,

▲ On March 15, 1956, the musical *My Fair Lady* opened on Broadway in New York City. The production, starring Julie Andrews as Eliza Doolittle and Rex Harrison as Henry Higgins, received rave reviews. *My Fair Lady* went on to be the longest-running Broadway musical to date, with a run of more than six years and an audience of almost 4 million people. Movie rights to the play were sold to Hollywood for more than $5 million.

Based on George Bernard Shaw's play *Pygmalion,* the musical changed the play's ending in favor of a 1950s-style happy ending.

GRACE KELLY'S STORYBOOK ROMANCE

Wedding bells rang for actress Grace Kelly and Prince Rainier III of Monaco on April 19, 1956. The wedding received much attention because the bride and groom were both popular public figures. Rainier had been prince of Monaco since 1949, and Kelly had become a celebrated actress after her first motion picture in 1951.

"without quite knowing what it is their kids are up to, are worried that it's something they shouldn't be." That new music was rock and roll.

New Technologies and New Markets

During the 1950s huge changes took place in the music world. The long-playing record, or LP, was developed by Dr. Peter Goldmark in 1948. LPs were cheaper and played much longer than the old "78s," and they gave better sound reproduction. Stereo records hit the market in 1958. Enthusiastic teenage consumers bought "45s," or singles, by the hundreds of thousands.

Those purchases were fueled by radio. By 1950 television's amazing success had forced radio to shift from network-produced shows to primarily news and music programming to survive. Independent radio stations around the country experimented with new

▶ Energetic performers like Little Richard (Richard Penniman) and his songs "Tutti Frutti" and "Long Tall Sally" set the tone of rock and roll.

formats. Local disk jockeys played an increasingly important role as personalities in the studio. Radios became standard equipment in cars to entertain both commuters and teenagers.

As African-Americans continued to migrate from the rural South to the large northern cities, more radio stations began to cater to black listeners. Before the mid-1940s, rhythm and blues music (R&B) had not been widely available to whites. By 1950 anyone could spin a radio dial and hear R&B. In 1953 even white disk jockeys like Alan Freed in Cleveland began to air black music. Freed played an important role in attracting white teenagers to R&B.

R&B Crosses Over

Major record producers saw the growing success of R&B songs on "race records" that were marketed for black listeners. These producers issued "cover versions" of these songs recorded by white artists. These white versions made the songs easier for white audiences to accept. Furthermore, the R&B influences they heard were the seeds of the developing style called rock and roll.

The 1955 release of Bill Haley's "Rock Around the Clock" was an important moment for white rock and roll. Listeners loved its driving rhythm and catchy lyrics. In its simplicity, the song seemed to speak directly to teenagers' energy and sense of rebellion.

Elvis Presley was the first superstar of rock and roll. He brought a unique personality to music and became a new type of cultural hero with a following of hysterical teenage fans. His country-and-western background paved the way for other "rockabilly" (rock and roll and hillbilly) artists such as the Everly Brothers. His hip movements on stage suggested a sexuality that outraged many parents. But his fans adored him.

Musical Generation Gap

The success of rock and roll was largely the result of the rise of the numbers and status of teenagers in the 1950s. As a result of the Baby Boom, record numbers of young people were reaching junior high and high school age. They

Elvis Presley: The King of Rock and Roll

In the 1950s a young man from Tupelo, Mississippi, set the music industry on its ear. He also set hearts on fire all over the world.

When Elvis Presley appeared on the scene, he was like no entertainer before him. A white man from the South, he sang music written by blacks. In 1954 Elvis's first record was a song called "That's All Right, Mama." When a Memphis radio sta-tion played it, the disk jockey called Elvis into the station to prove to the studio audience that the singer was white. The station got so many calls that the disk jockey played the song 13 times in a row. It was a landmark event in the birth of rock and roll.

In 1955 a successful promoter by the name of Colonel Tom Parker began to manage Elvis's career. One year later, Elvis produced his first major hit "Heartbreak Hotel." It was the first of 45 records that sold more than a million copies each. Other hit records included "Hound Dog," "Don't Be Cruel," and "All Shook Up."

Elvis shocked adults and inspired the young with his music and his open sexuality. He was a rebel who wore his hair and his sideburns long. His lips were always in a sexy pout or a nasty sneer. He was full of energy, and when he sang, his whole body wiggled. The way he moved his hips was considered indecent by some. The first time Elvis appeared on *The Ed Sullivan Show,* a popular TV variety show, he was shown only from the waist up. People called him "Elvis the Pelvis" or the "Atomic-Powered Singer."

Wherever Elvis appeared, women screamed and some even fainted. Popular magazines ran articles like "Why Elvis Is Every Girl's Idol." Fan clubs sprang up everywhere. And it was not long before Hollywood caught on. In 1956 Elvis made his motion picture debut in *Love Me Tender.* He starred in 32 more box-office hits, which drew audiences well into the 1960s.

In 1958, at the height of his popularity, Elvis was drafted by the Army. The draft board broke the hearts of women everywhere. When he returned to public life in 1960, he continued his career. Although much of the hysteria had died while Elvis was in the service, he continued to draw huge audiences, and he stayed popular long after his death in 1977.

filled their after-school hours watching television or listening to music. The heavy beat and simple melodies of rock and roll struck a chord with young people. Furthermore, the music was increasingly geared toward them. Typical rock and roll lyrics communicated basic teenage interests: young love, adolescent problems, and cars. Many rock and roll stars were also teenagers themselves.

By the late 1950s, pop music had split in two: adult pop and teenage pop. A "generation gap"

was opening, although it would not be fully evident until the 1960s. Adults preferred to listen to singers from the Big Band era who were now singing on their own. Frank Sinatra, who burst onto the music scene in the early 1940s, was still riding high. Perry Como developed a mellow, homey musical style to deliver ballads and love songs. Nat "King" Cole began performing at clubs in Harlem and soon became popular with white audiences. But the kids were listening to loud rock and roll.

Jazz Breaks Away to Bebop

Charlie "Bird" Parker. Thelonious Monk. Dizzy Gillespie. These geniuses of jazz were the spirit of the bebop era at its peak in the 1940s and 1950s.

The bebop style began when a few black jazz musicians, tired of playing in the rigid style of the big bands, started playing in after-hours "jam sessions." They used loosely constructed musical scores or no scores at all. The bebop group usually consisted of a saxophone, a trumpet, a piano, a string bass, and drums. Bebop's harmonies sounded unusual, and its tempos were faster than usual jazz tempos. The rhythm was more irregular. The piano supplied the chords, while the string bass formed the core of the rhythm section.

Bebop reached the public in the 1950s the same way

jazz had always reached it, in nightclubs and on records. Because bebop combos were small, each musician had to be excellent. The players showed off their skill in long solos.

▼ ▼ ▼

Charlie "Bird" Parker. Thelonious Monk. Dizzy Gillespie. These geniuses of jazz were the spirit of the bebop era at its peak in the 1940s and 1950s.

Charlie Parker, an alto saxophonist, started out in a big band. In 1945, while playing in New York's 52nd Street jazz clubs, he and Dizzy Gillespie made the first significant bebop recordings. Gillespie's trademark was his unusual trumpet. Its bell pointed upward at a 45-degree angle. In the 1940s he played with prominent big bands. With Parker and pi-

anist Thelonious Monk, he helped create the bebop style. Monk did most of his work as a soloist or as the leader of small groups. His compositions are still considered standards. His unusual harmonies made him a principal influence on **avant-garde** jazz.

Other jazz greats of the era developed their own influential styles. Educated at Juilliard, Miles Davis joined Parker's band in 1945. He later formed his own jazz group and established several important jazz styles. He made some of the first jazz recordings in the style called "cool." John Coltrane, tenor and soprano sax player and composer, played with Miles Davis in the 1950s. He later formed his own band in the 1960s. He became a leader of the jazz movement called "New Wave."

THE CULTURE OF CONFORMITY

In the 1950s, the incredible popularity of television was changing people's habits. It became Americans' main source for news, although newspaper readership did not decline significantly. But television did not stop Americans from reading books. They especially liked the paperbacks that were sold everywhere: in supermarkets, in drugstores, at train stations, and in airports.

Suburban Reading

As they always have, American readers looked for escape in the popular forms of writing in the era. The means of escape, however, reflected their changing world and lifestyles. Westerns and romances became ever more popular, and urban detective stories and science fiction gained large followings. In fact, Americans consumed these kinds of books in increasing numbers. People bought detective thrillers by Mickey Spillane and space adventures by Isaac Asimov. They devoured Grace Metalious's gossipy *Peyton Place*. They also preferred books that reflected the attitudes of suburban America's "consensus society." Those books focused on family needs, problems, and values. Jean Kerr's *Please Don't Eat the Daisies*, also a best-seller, was a mildly sarcastic account about being a homemaker and mother in the 1950s. Norman Vincent Peale's *The Power of Positive Thinking* was one book among many offering advice on how to get ahead in America's success-oriented culture.

The Baby Boom generated interest in children and the world in which they were growing up. Under the name of Dr. Seuss, Theodor Geisel wrote many children's books that became best-sellers. Mothers read *The 500 Hats of Bartholomew Cubbins* to their children, and the kids read *The Cat in the Hat* and *Green Eggs and Ham* by themselves. Other easy-to-read books soon followed, as parents urged their children to get a head start before entering kindergarten.

Television host Art Linkletter's *Kids Say the Darndest Things*, with short, amusing stories about cute youngsters, hit the best-seller list. So did Pat Boone's *'Twixt Twelve and Twenty,* in which the clean-cut popular singer offered wholesome advice and middle-class values to teenagers.

The Postwar World

Much popular reading material addressed serious themes in the postwar, Cold War world. Some books presented the grim realities of World War II. For example, *Anne Frank: The Diary of a Young Girl* described a young girl's terrors and trials in hiding during the Nazi occupation. Norman Mailer's *The Naked and the Dead*, James Jones's *From Here to Eternity*, and Herman Wouk's *The Caine Mutiny* all dealt with the realistic aspects of war. *I Led Three Lives*, Herbert Philbrick's book about communist spying, kept people's Cold War fears alive. Eugene Burdick and Harvey Wheeler's novel *Fail-Safe* depicted the possible scenario of an accidental atomic war.

THE PEANUTS GANG

In 1950 Charles Schulz created *Peanuts*, a comic strip that uses a group of children to comment on life's contradictions and complexities. The cast of characters began with Charlie Brown and his dog Snoopy and Linus and his sister Lucy. Schulz based the character of Charlie Brown loosely on himself. Although Schulz may have viewed himself as a born loser as a child, he has achieved success as an adult. His cartoon now appears in almost 2,000 newspapers in the United States and Canada alone. The *Peanuts* gang has also starred in several television specials.

NEW WORDS
catch-22

hi-fi

rock and roll

situation comedy

stereophonic sound

theater-in-the-round

A number of social scientists and novelists addressed the problems of the consensus society. David Riesman's *The Lonely Crowd*, Vance Packard's *The Status Seekers*, and William H. Whyte's *The Organization Man* all attempted to explain the pressures of middle-class society and how they led people to conform. John Updike's novel *Rabbit, Run* gave a fictionalized account of the hollowness of suburban culture. Jack Kerouac's *On the Road* expressed the urge of the "Beat Generation" of writers to escape the constraints of conventional society.

Black novelist James Baldwin, in *Go Tell It on the Mountain*, *The Fire Next Time*, and *Notes of a Native Son*, expressed rage at having been excluded by the dominant society. This anger was echoed in the poetry of Gwendolyn Brooks, who wrote about the suffering and resentments of urban blacks. These works called attention to the fact that most African-Americans were living on the dangerous margins of a society that claimed to be democratic and humane.

The works of Saul Bellow, Bernard Malamud, and Philip Roth addressed an American Jewish culture increasingly aware of itself and an American society increasingly aware of its diversity. Bellow's many novels, including *Seize the Day* and *The Adventures of Augie March*, reflected his background as the son of Russian Jews from a Polish Chicago neighborhood. Malamud wrote mainly about Jews growing up in the neighborhoods of New York City. Roth's *Goodbye Columbus* was a collection of stories that parodied urban and suburban Jewish life.

Spirit of the Age

Although much in American life had changed significantly in the 1950s, respect for religion and the Bible remained popular. The Revised Standard Version was published and became a best-seller along with the King James Version. At the same time, however, some people's outlook became increasingly distrustful of human nature and motives. Many people read the **existentialist** works of Albert Camus and Jean-Paul Sartre. There was a growing gulf between the mass of the people and intellectuals. The middle class was comfortable and hopeful; it treasured traditional values. Intellectuals felt despair and hopelessness.

Popular Books, 1946–1963

Year	Title	Author
1946	The King's General	Daphne du Maurier
1947	The Miracle of the Bells	Russell Janney
1948	The Big Fisherman	Lloyd C. Douglas
1949	The Egyptian	Mika Waltari
1950	The Cardinal	Henry Morton Robinson
1951	From Here to Eternity	James Jones
1952	The Silver Chalice	Thomas B. Costain
1953	The Robe	Lloyd C. Douglas
1954	Not as a Stranger	Morton Thompson
1955	Marjorie Morningstar	Herman Wouk
1956	Don't Go Near the Water	William Brinkley
1957	By Love Possessed	James Gould Cozzens
1958	Doctor Zhivago	Boris Pasternak
1959	Exodus	Leon Uris
1960	Advise and Consent	Allen Drury
1961	The Agony and the Ecstasy	Irving Stone
1962	Ship of Fools	Katherine Anne Porter
1963	The Shoes of the Fisherman	Morris L. West

THE ARTS GO ABSTRACT

As America's cultural influence spread worldwide through the mass media, New York became the center of modern art. Artists and intellectuals searching for the soul of 1950s America sneered at the shallow materialism and "togetherness" that they saw in the prosperous middle class. The avant-garde in literature, music, art, dance, and architecture began looking for depth and complexity in abstract forms and random patterns. Their attitudes affected the literary, artistic, and scholarly works of the 1950s.

A painting style known as "abstract expressionism" arose in the United States and set the tone for the art world. Artists such as Jackson Pollock, Willem de Kooning, and Mark Rothko experimented with technique, color, and form rather than depicting objects. Abstract works challenged people's ideas about what art is, and some had trouble understanding and appreciating these paintings. They asked, "Can this be art if I can't even tell what it's supposed to be?"

Similarly, classical composers of the postwar era rejected fixed ideas about melody, rhythm, and form in music. American composers Elliott Carter, John Cage, and Milton Babbitt used free-form styles that were difficult to play and often difficult for listeners to follow. Cage, for example, explored the outer boundaries of what was normally thought of as music by incorporating many nonmusical sounds—like banging doors—into

his work. One of his pieces, called *4'33"* consisted of four minutes and 33 seconds of silence.

Dance became more abstract, too. Earlier in the century Martha Graham had helped to create modern dance, developing powerfully expressive movements. Throughout the 1940s, 1950s, and 1960s, she illustrated American themes, like the pioneering spirit in *Appalachian Spring* and southwestern culture in *El Penitente*. She also developed expressive dances that explored universal psychological states found in the myths of various cultures.

Under Walter Gropius, Le Corbusier, and Ludwig Miës van der Rohe, the International Style dominated 1950s architecture. Following Miës's principle that "less is more," these architects proceeded to make modern forms out of modern materials. Their boxlike structures of steel beams and glass-curtain walls have remained icons of modern skyscraper architecture.

▲ American artist Jackson Pollock poured and spattered the paint over his canvases, a process he called "Action Painting."

LEONARD BERNSTEIN MAKES MUSIC

The year 1943 brought fame to Leonard Bernstein. Having just been named assistant conductor of the New York Philharmonic, he was suddenly called on to substitute for the scheduled conductor. Bernstein found himself conducting a nationally broadcast concert. His much-praised performance was the foundation of his esteemed career.

During the 1950s Bernstein was a musical dynamo. He wrote the music for several musicals, including *West Side Story* and *Candide*. In 1958 he became the Philharmonic's first American-born musical director. He left the orchestra 11 years later to concentrate on composing.

SPORTS AND LEISURE

Jackie Robinson was more than just a ballplayer—although he was an excellent one. Robinson was a cause. The first black in the modern major leagues, he ushered in a new era in sports and society.

Robinson had a tremendous impact because sports were growing in importance. People had more money to spend and more time to spend it. Americans joined softball and bowling leagues, took up tennis and golf, joined swim clubs, and learned to ice-skate. Meanwhile, children played on Little League baseball and Pop Warner football teams.

But Americans did not just play sports. They became eager spectators in record numbers. They attended baseball, basketball, hockey, and football games. They watched ten-

AT A GLANCE

- ▶ The National Pastime
- ▶ Reaching New Heights
- ▶ Football Comes of Age
- ▶ Soccer Invades America
- ▶ The Greening of America
- ▶ Breaking Records
- ▶ It Can Be Yours

nis matches. They lined the fairways at golf tournaments.

Sports and television turned out to be perfect together. Americans began staying home to watch their favorite athletes and teams on television. As professional sports expanded after the war, the fans followed them into the living room as well as into the stands. With the addition of big advertising dollars, television and big-time sports helped each other grow in size and in wealth.

Television accelerated the twentieth-century trend of the rise of professionalism in American sports. But the increased TV coverage of sports helped amateur and college athletics as well. Whether played or watched, sports became an ever more dominant part of American life and leisure time.

DATAFILE

Sports

World records as of 1955	Men	Women
Track and field		
100-yd. dash	9.3″	10.4″
Mile	3′57.9″	4′45.0″
High jump	7.0 ft.	5.7 ft.
Swimming		
100-m. freestyle	55.8″	1′06.8″

Leisure

	1946	1963
Average workweek	40.3 hrs.	40.5 hrs.
Attendance		
Baseball (major leagues)	17.8 mil.	20.7 mil.
Football (NFL)	1.7 mil.	4.2 mil.
National parks	8.9 mil.	33.4 mil.
Bicycle sales	2.9 mil.	3.8 mil.

PAYDIRT!
Attendance at NFL Football Games, 1946–1963

Source: National Football League.

THE NATIONAL PASTIME

Baseball's popularity reached a new high in the years after the Second World War. It was an era that saw important changes and gave rise to some of the game's greatest legends.

The most important change in the game was the end of segregation. From the turn of the century until 1946 none of the major-league teams included black players. Blacks were limited to the Negro leagues. They played against each other mostly, occasionally meeting a white team in an exhibition game. Because they never had a chance to compete in major-league baseball, many great black players never received the national recognition they deserved. The long list of Negro-league stars includes such legends as Josh Gibson and Satchel Paige.

In 1946 the Brooklyn Dodgers broke baseball's color barrier by signing Jackie Robinson for the 1947 season. In the summer of 1947 the American League's first black player—the Cleveland Indians' Larry Doby—made his debut. Both Robinson and Doby played well. Equally important, they withstood the abuse of fans—and sometimes even that of their white teammates. As a result of their success the door opened wide for other black players. Willie Mays, who joined the New York Giants in 1951, is another black baseball pioneer who quickly rose to stardom. The game had been transformed, and nearly everyone agreed it was better for the change.

Jackie Robinson Makes Baseball History

◀ The first black All-Stars (1949): (from left) Roy Campanella, Larry Doby, Don Newcombe, and Jackie Robinson

Baseball's opening day, April 18, 1946, was especially exciting. It was the start of the first minor-league season since the end of the war. But that was not all. When Jackie Robinson came to bat, he would be the first black man in the twentieth century to play in organized minor-league baseball.

"This in a way is another Emancipation Day for the Negro race," Baz O'Meara wrote in Montreal's *Daily Star*. Wendell Smith, the black sportswriter of the Pittsburgh *Courier*, reported, "Everyone sensed the significance of the occasion as Robinson . . . marched with the Montreal team to deep center field for the raising of the Stars and Stripes and the 'Star Spangled Banner.'"

Six months before, General Manager Branch Rickey of the Brooklyn Dodgers had surprised America by signing Robinson to play for the Dodgers' top farm club. Everyone wondered whether Rickey had been wise. Some said that players and fans would be against this move to integrate baseball. Until then, like all black baseball players of that era, Robinson had played for a team in the Negro leagues.

On his first time up that day, Robinson felt nervous. He later said that his hands seemed "too moist to grip the bat." But in his second at-bat, Robinson hit a three-run homer, and baseball history was changed forever.

Rickey brought Robinson, at age 28, to Brooklyn the next year. He was an immediate success. He hit for a .297 average, scored 125 runs, led the league with 29 stolen bases, and helped the Dodgers to win their first pennant since 1941. He was named Rookie of the Year.

Later, Robinson helped lead the Dodgers to six World Series appearances in ten years.

In 1949 Robinson was named the league's Most Valuable Player, batting .342, with 37 stolen bases, 122 runs, 124 runs batted in, and 203 hits. He was an outstanding fielder as well. Usually a second baseman, he led the league in fielding average at his position three times. In 1962 he became the first black elected to the Baseball Hall of Fame.

An all-around athlete, Robinson had been a four-sport star at UCLA. But Rickey chose Robinson to break baseball's color barrier as much for his character as for his skill. Intelligent, articulate, proud, and poised, Robinson proved to be the ideal person to stand up to the scrutiny—and the bigotry—of American baseball players and fans.

Admitting black players into the major leagues opened up baseball to a wider range of talent, changed the style of play, and gave the sport a broader appeal.

Baseball Goes Coast to Coast

The second big change in baseball in this era was major-league expansion. Since 1903 the same 16 teams had played in the same ten cities, primarily in the East. But now there were more fans living in new population centers, especially in the Midwest and West. In the mid-1950s three longtime losers went to other cities, hoping to find new fans. In 1953 the Boston Braves moved to Milwaukee. The next year the St. Louis Browns became the Baltimore Orioles. And in 1955 the Philadelphia Athletics moved to Kansas City.

The big shake-up, however, came in 1958. Two winning teams with loyal fans—the Dodgers and the Giants—left New York for Los Angeles and San Francisco. Now major-league baseball was truly a national game.

To take further advantage of new markets, baseball owners decided to add more teams. The American League moved first. In 1961 its owners placed a team in Los Angeles (the Angels) and moved the Washington Senators to Minneapolis–St. Paul (where they became the Twins), then added a new Senators team in Washington. The National League followed the next year with teams in Houston (now the Astros) and New York (the Mets). The New York team aimed to recapture Dodger and Giant fans.

Improved air travel made coast-to-coast play practical. Playing more games at night, which increased attendance and produced greater ticket revenues, helped fund expansion. But the biggest source of new money was television. Baseball signed a $6 million deal in 1950 for television rights to the World Series. Teams signed their own contracts with local television stations to earn even more money. And a national network began showing the "game of the week" each Saturday.

Expansion of the major leagues and television coverage of big-league games took their toll on the minor leagues, however. Within a decade, the number of minor-league teams was cut in half. Attendance at games dropped by more than 25 million. Sportswriters criticized the major-league team owners for hurting the minors. But the demand for major-league play—live and on television—continued to grow.

The Team at the Top

Through all of these changes, one thing appeared constant. The American League's New York Yankees dominated postwar baseball. From 1949 to 1963 they won ten league pennants and won the World Series seven times.

Part of the credit for the team's amazing winning streak goes to Charles Dillon "Casey" Stengel, the manager from 1949 to 1960. Before joining the Yankees, Stengel had had a reputation as a clown. In nine years as manager of the Brooklyn Dodgers and the Boston Braves, he had never had a winning season. That changed with the Yankees.

The Yankees' lineup certainly contributed to the team's success. It included such baseball legends as shortstop Phil Rizzuto, pitcher Whitey Ford, catcher Lawrence "Yogi" Berra, and center fielders

THE WORLD SERIES ON TELEVISION

In 1947 almost 4 million people watched the World Series in their homes when the fall classic was broadcast on television for the first time. All three networks—ABC, CBS, and NBC—carried the games, which matched the New York Yankees and the Brooklyn Dodgers. Gillette and Ford paid $65,000 to sponsor the historic broadcasts.

MICKEY MANTLE AND ROGER MARIS

Mickey Mantle played baseball with the New York Yankees from 1951 through 1968, his entire major-league career. In that time he became one of baseball's leading home-run hitters, hitting 536. He hit a record 18 more in World Series play.

In 1961 Mantle was upstaged by the remarkable summer of teammate Roger Maris. Maris entered the record books that year by hitting 61 homers, one more than Babe Ruth's single-season record set in 1927. Mantle finished that season with 54; the 115 home runs between the teammates set a new two-man standard.

Joe DiMaggio and Mickey Mantle. Berra (in 1951, 1954, and 1955) and Mantle (in 1956, 1957, and 1962) were each named the American League's Most Valuable Player three times.

Stengel's teams of the 1950s seemed unstoppable. But the winning streak proved that it might be possible to have too much of a good thing. Because many people like to root for the underdog, the overpowering Yankees became the most-hated team in baseball. Crowds booed when they won, and attendance dropped at Yankee Stadium—even after the Dodgers and Giants had left town.

Basketball

REACHING NEW HEIGHTS

In the postwar era many changes took place in organized basketball, beginning with the formation of a new professional league, the National Basketball Association (NBA). Very tall players in the NBA and colleges attracted worldwide attention and changed the nature of the sport forever.

In addition, pro ball quickly became integrated. In 1950 the NBA's Boston Celtics drafted Chuck Cooper, who became the first black to play on a white professional team. In that year Nat "Sweetwater" Clifton left the Harlem Globetrotters, an all-black professional touring team, and signed with the NBA's New York Knickerbockers. Many other black players were then signed by NBA teams throughout the country.

College basketball underwent changes as well. Black college enrollment rose after World War II, and more blacks were recruited to play basketball. In parts of the South, however, some college teams remained all white even after their schools had begun to desegregate in the late 1950s.

Pro Basketball Grows

Professional basketball experienced real success in 1946, when teams began competing in big-city arenas. That year the Basketball Association of America (BAA) was formed. Two years later four top teams left the National Basketball League (NBL) and joined the BAA. In 1949 the two competing leagues merged to form the NBA. The NBA introduced the 24-second clock and instituted a new player draft in which it signed the best college players for teams. Basketball then began its greatest growth spurt, both in popularity and in the size of its players.

George Mikan, a 6-foot 10-inch center for the Minneapolis Lakers, became basketball's first dominant "big man." He led his team to five NBA championships. But the biggest star was Wilt "The Stilt" Chamberlain. At 7 feet 1 inch, Chamberlain was so tall that, at first, some people complained that his height would ruin the game. A star in high school, he became an All-American at the University of Kansas in 1957. He left Kansas to play with the Globetrotters. After a year he went to the NBA, where he eventually played for three teams, the Philadelphia Warriors, the Philadelphia 76ers, and the Los Angeles Lakers. Chamberlain's scoring and rebounding were legendary. He led the league in both for many years.

Two more stars joined basketball's ranks in the 1950s. Both were a part of the Boston Celtics dynasty. Bill Russell revolutionized basketball with his defensive skills and won the Most Valuable Player award five times. Bob Cousy, a superb ballhandler and passer, helped the Celtics win six NBA championships in the 1950s and 1960s. In 1957 he was named the Most Valuable Player in basketball.

Hoops a Hit at All Levels

As basketball became more popular throughout the country, new, larger college arenas accommodated more fans. Recruiting efforts by the NBA were increased. Games were televised, and increased attendance and television commercials earned the sport ever larger revenues.

From cities to small towns, young people played basketball, using everything from regulation backboards and hoops to bushel baskets wired to fences or barn doors. Scouts visited high schools to recruit promising players for men's college teams. Girls and women played women's basketball in increasing numbers as well.

Football

FOOTBALL COMES OF AGE

While the United States was at war, many colleges had to restrict or suspend their athletic programs. After the war, a flood of new play-

ers arrived on campuses, and people flocked to see their favorite college football teams play. Notre Dame, Michigan, Army, Southern California, Ohio State, Pittsburgh, and the Ivy League schools all drew big crowds. In the late 1950s, professional football entertained fans on weekends in more and more American living rooms. In fact, television coverage contributed greatly to the increase in popularity of professional football.

Big Teams, Big Stars, Big Games

After the war, a new professional league, the All-American Football Conference (AAFC), was organized for the 1946 season. All-American teams were located in Brooklyn, Buffalo, Chicago, Cleveland, Los Angeles, Miami, New York, and San Francisco.

◄ Wilt Chamberlain (with ball) squares off against longtime rival Bill Russell, the 6-foot 10-inch center for the Boston Celtics. While Chamberlain reached new scoring heights, Russell was a master of defense and the blocked shot. The arrival of George Mikan, Chamberlain, Russell, and other giant centers led the NBA to widen the lane under the basket.

CHAMBERLAIN HITS THE CENTURY MARK

In the 1961–1962 season, Wilt Chamberlain did the impossible. He, alone, scored 100 points in a single game. He also led the league in scoring that year, averaging 50 points a game.

SPORTS ILLUSTRATED HITS THE STANDS

In 1954 Henry R. Luce, publisher of *Time* and *Life* magazines, launched a new weekly magazine aimed at American sports fans. On August 16 the first issue of *Sports Illustrated* went on sale for 25 cents.

In the years that followed, the National Football League (NFL) and the AAFC spent large amounts of money trying to outbid each other for college stars and to lure players from one league to the other. Finally, before the 1950 season, the two leagues agreed to a merger. The NFL absorbed the Cleveland Browns and the San Francisco 49ers. The Browns won the first championship of the combined leagues.

Postwar interest in pro football grew as changes in the rules made for a faster-paced, more exciting game. The new rules allowed for more scoring. Unlimited substitutions let players be brought on and off the field as often as necessary. As players became specialized, the days of the two-way player—who played both offense and defense— disappeared.

Football became more of a passing game, and passing quarterbacks became the big stars. Otto Graham, quarterback for the Cleveland Browns from 1946 to 1955, threw for 174 touchdowns. He also ran for 46 more. From 1956 to 1960 Johnny Unitas led the Baltimore Colts to two NFL championships. He played for the Colts until 1973.

Althea Gibson Breaks a Barrier

"I have sat in on many dramatic moments in sports, but few were more thrilling than Miss Gibson's performance . . . not because great tennis was played . . . but because of the great try by this lonely, and nervous, colored girl," observed David Eisenberg in the New York *Journal-American.* The year was 1950, and the match was the outdoor championships at Forest Hills, New York. Althea Gibson was the first black to compete in this previously all-white, top-level event.

African-American players had often tried to enter the championships. But clubs had managed to keep them out by answering their entries in the same way: "Refused. Insufficient informa-tion." By 1950 increasing pressure to include blacks forced the U.S. Lawn Tennis Association to admit Gibson as a contestant.

She lost the match at Forest Hills, partly because of a rain delay. "The delay was the worst thing that could have happened to me," Gibson later wrote in her autobiography. "It gave me a whole evening—and the next morning—to think about the match. I was a nervous wreck." But that match was only the beginning for this talented 21-year-old Florida A. & M. student.

Gibson went on to win the Italian championship in 1956 and again in 1957, when she also won at Wimbledon and at the U.S. Open championships. She again won at Wimbledon and the U.S. Open in 1958 and was ranked first in the world among women players in 1957 and 1958. Her courage and competitive spirit helped to change tennis by opening it up to all talented players.

Teams got tougher, crowds got bigger, and the stars got stronger and faster. The Baltimore Colts and the New York Giants played for the championship twice, in 1958 and 1959. The first nationally televised game was the 1958 championship. The television audience saw a thrilling contest that the Colts won in overtime.

From 1959 to 1967 the Green Bay Packers dominated pro football. They won 89 games, lost 29, and tied 4. The Packers' coach, Vince Lombardi, used a new system of tough discipline with his players. Other coaches soon adopted his methods, which became the standard way of training football players. The Packers took five NFL titles through 1967 and handily won the first two Super Bowls, in 1967 and 1968.

Superstar Jim Brown captured the attention of the football world in the 1950s and 1960s. His speed, size, and strength made him football's foremost running back. Many experts still call him the greatest running back of all time. Drafted by the Cleveland Browns, he led the NFL in rushing in his rookie year, 1957, and for seven of the next eight years. He set records for yards rushing in a career (a record that was not broken until 1984) and touchdowns in a career. He never missed a game because of injury. He was inducted into both the College Football and Professional Football halls of fame.

Move Over, Baseball

Alvin Ray "Pete" Rozelle became NFL commissioner in 1960. Under his guidance and leadership, professional football became the most popular big-money sport in the United States. Rozelle recognized that good television coverage was the key to making big football even bigger. In 1961 he arranged to get federal laws modified so that a single television network would have broadcast rights to cover all the league games. Football **franchises** that had once cost $100 were now worth millions.

In 1959 a group of millionaires formed the American Football League (AFL). Once again the NFL faced stiff competition as the AFL lured talented college players by making them large financial offers. The two leagues would eventually merge in the 1960s.

College Ball Stays Strong

The best postwar college teams were Notre Dame, Army, Michigan, and the University of Oklahoma. Oklahoma was national champion in 1950, 1955, and 1956. They had a 47-game victory streak from 1953 to 1957.

In the years following World War II, an informal working arrangement emerged between the National Collegiate Athletic Association (NCAA) and the NFL. The NFL agreed not to draft undergraduates, thus protecting the college market for players.

Soccer

SOCCER INVADES AMERICA

Soccer had long been the most popular sport in both Europe and South America. Star soccer players became celebrities for life. Since

AT THE SUMMIT

New Zealander Sir Edmund Hillary and his Nepalese guide Tenzing Norgay became the first people to climb Mount Everest, the world's tallest mountain. They reached the summit of the Himalayan peak on May 29, 1953.

▼ One of the best rivalries in professional golf began in 1962 when Jack Nicklaus (right) beat Arnold Palmer (left) to win the U.S. Open. Palmer won the Masters and British Open that year. Another rising star, South African Gary Player, crouches between the once and future champions. Player won the 1962 PGA title.

1930 the top professional teams from around the world have competed every four years for the World Cup championship.

Soccer arrived in the United States during the late nineteenth century. However, its popularity really took off after 1959, when the NCAA recognized it as an official collegiate sport with a national championship tournament.

Pelé, the world-famous soccer star, also deserves credit for making soccer more popular in the United States. From 1957 to 1974 Pelé played for the Brazilian national team. In 1958, 1962, and 1970, he led them to victory in the World Cup.

Pelé's spectacular soccer playing made him an international star. He inspired many young people to try the game at the amateur level. They found it easy to learn,

less injurious than American football, and equally enjoyable for both boys and girls. In the 1950s and 1960s amateur soccer became the fastest-growing sport in the United States at the amateur level.

Golf

THE GREENING OF AMERICA

The first American golfers teed off in 1888, but it was not until after World War II that the game became a major sport and popular pastime. As long as golf was largely the domain of the country-club well-to-do, the popularity of the professional tour was limited. In the 1950s golf grew in appeal. Stimulating that growth was interest in the striking individuals who made up the golfing world. Another spur to that growth was television.

The first stand-out golfer to attract attention was Ben Hogan. Hogan had already begun to achieve his promise as a golfer by the time of a near-fatal auto accident in 1949. He had won the Professional Golfers Association (PGA) title twice and the U.S. Open once. After the accident Hogan was told he would probably never walk again, much less play golf. A year later, still limping from his injuries, he won the U.S. Open again. He went on to win several more titles, including a trio of major championships—the Masters and the U.S. and British Opens—in 1953.

Hogan's comeback made him a hero and helped capture popular attention to his game. Other greats of the era were known as much for personality as for skill on the course. "Slammin" Sammy Snead, for instance, was famous for his long drives and quick wit. As important to popularizing the game were celebrity amateur golfers. Hollywood stars like Bing Crosby and Bob Hope showed their devotion to the game by sponsoring tournaments. The most important weekend golfer lived in the White House for eight years. President Eisenhower's obvious attachment to the game may have encouraged others to give in to the growing urge to hit the golf course.

While the weekend game was moving from private to public courses, television was turning golf into a popular spectator sport. Television brought to the general public the dramatic moments and appealing personalities of golf. Young Arnold Palmer provided a great deal of both, and his televised feats brought the game home to everyone. His habit of falling behind and then making a late charge endeared him to many fans. So, too, did the whole range of emotions he showed after winning a tournament or falling just short. He developed a literal following at every tournament in "Arnie's Army," who marched faithfully behind him around the course.

By the early 1960s another star who would challenge Arnold Palmer loomed on the horizon. In 1962 Jack Nicklaus beat Palmer to become the youngest player to win the U.S. Open since 1923. The next year he became the youngest player to win the Masters Tournament. Nicklaus was about to embark on an outstanding career.

Other Sports

BREAKING RECORDS

The postwar years saw many long-standing records shattered and new ones set. Roger Bannister made track history in 1954, when he became the first to run a mile in less than four minutes. Rod Laver, one of the all-time tennis greats, won four Wimbledon singles titles, two U.S. Open championships, and three Australian and two French titles between 1959 and 1969. The first player since 1938 to win these four championships in a single year, he is still the only player to win the Grand Slam of tennis twice (1962 and 1969).

Humans were not the only athletes to set new records. Citation was the first horse to win more than $1 million in his career. In 1948 the three-year-old thoroughbred won the Kentucky Derby, the

BETTER VAULTING THROUGH CHEMISTRY

In February 1962, U.S. Marine Corporal John Uesles set a pole-vaulting record of 16 feet ¼ inch. The next day he broke his own record by ½ inch. Almost three months later Marine Lieutenant Dave Tork set a new record of 16 feet 2 inches.

Both of these vaulters used poles made with fiberglass, instead of bamboo or aluminum, sparking much controversy. Don Bragg, who had held the vaulting record before February 1962, objected. He believed that fiberglass poles were more flexible than other poles, giving competitors an unfair advantage. Today, almost all pole-vaulters use poles made with fiberglass.

Preakness, and the Belmont Stakes. This feat earned him the Triple Crown of horse racing.

In 1956 Rocky Marciano retired from boxing, the only undefeated heavyweight champion ever. He had won 42 professional bouts and defended his title six times. Cassius Clay (now Muhammad Ali) became famous as the Olympic light-heavyweight champion in 1960, and he turned pro later that year. In the decades ahead, he would become the most celebrated sports figure in the world.

The Montreal Canadiens dominated postwar pro hockey. They won the Stanley Cup five times in a row from 1956 to 1960.

Rebels Without a Cause

▲ James Dean

Holden Caulfield was an unlikely hero for a whole generation of American adolescents. He was a 16-year-old reject from private schools—a character in J. D. Salinger's 1951 novel *The Catcher in the Rye.* The restless Caulfield did not trust adults, hated their way of life, and felt that he did not belong. To many adults' dismay, a lot of American youth in the 1950s identified with Holden Caulfield.

As adults were making life orderly and comfortable in the suburbs, teenagers were hatching a revolution in style and values. No longer satisfied with the adults' "status quo," they found new heroes in young actors like Marlon Brando and James Dean. Brando sometimes played the part of a "hood" or motorcycle-gang leader. With blue jeans and slicked-back hair, these characters snarled in defiance of the "establishment." Dean became the symbol of the wronged and misunderstood teenager. In his most famous movie, *Rebel Without a Cause,* he played a teenager who felt he could not fit into the comfortable, suburban adult world.

Fifties teens tended to be one of two types: the "clean-cut" boy or "girl next door," or the rebellious hood. Overall, American youth definitely had different values and different music. "Rock Around the Clock" was their new national anthem.

Leisure

IT CAN BE YOURS

In the 1950s fads and fancies reflected the life of suburban families. Television, the youth culture, and automobiles had a powerful impact on people's everyday life.

Children who were born after the war made up the first generation to be raised on television. The shows they watched spawned a whole new line of toys and games. Popular shows included Disney's *Davy Crockett,* which created a $100 million market for coonskin caps; *The Mickey Mouse Club,* which sold all kinds of Mickey-related clothing and gadgets; and *Howdy Doody.* Advertisers also cashed in on the appeal of these programs by running commercials during them for children's products, such as breakfast cereals and toys.

Scrabble and other family board games became very popular. In 1959 the Barbie doll came on the market. Other toys, like Slinky, Silly Putty, and Tonka toys, appeared. The big toy manufacturers,

like Mattel and Marx, became household names. Children also collected and traded comic books and baseball cards.

The carefree 1950s produced many fads. The Frisbee appeared in 1957 and the Hula Hoop in 1958. College students stuffed themselves into phone booths or Volkswagens for fun. Family lawn games like croquet, badminton, horseshoes, and tetherball became popular. And for the first time, people could capture their good times in instant Polaroid photos.

Cars and highways were changing the nation. Family recreation became more mobile. Millions of vacationers drove to national parks, ocean resorts, and amusement parks. Motels, roadside stands, and campgrounds sprang up. Disneyland opened in Anaheim, California, in 1955 and immediately drew big crowds.

The suburban middle class had to have the "musts" for home recreation: table tennis and billiard tables, swimming pools, and more. Suburbanites threw cocktail parties in the rec room or by the pool, or they invited friends over and barbecued.

Upwardly mobile Americans new to the middle class sought advice. "How are we supposed to behave?" "What are we supposed to think?" "What are our children supposed to be doing?" Ann Landers, "Dear Abby," and Amy Vanderbilt had all the answers to these questions and more.

In fashion, the postwar "New Look" from Paris set the tone with luxuriant dresses. Inexpensive copies hit the stores so that, for the first time, most women could afford the latest styles. Hemlines went up and down, and people bought and bought.

▲ No kid wanted to be the last to get the latest toy or gadget sweeping the country. After learning how to twist the plastic Hula Hoop around their waists (or arms or legs), kids tried to see how long they could keep it spinning. Following up on the 3-D movie craze, "Three Dimension Comics" gave the appearance of depth with special glasses.

DON'T BE A DRAG— JUST HANG LOOSE

The youth subculture of the postwar era used slang like never before. Here are a few terms:
   drag race (from a standing start)
   grounded (can't go out)
   hot rod ("souped-up" car)
   square (someone really out of it)
   passion pit (drive-in movie)
   wheels (car)

VOICES OF THE ERA

Joe Gillis: You used to be in pictures. You used to be big.

Norma Desmond: I am big. It's the pictures that got small.

—From the film *Sunset Boulevard,* 1950

Men have a much better time of it than women. For one thing, they marry later. For another thing, they die earlier.

—H. L. Mencken,
A Mencken Chrestomathy,
1949

I guess if I could choose one of the most important moments in my life, I would go back to 1947 in Yankee Stadium in New York City. It was the opening day of the world series, and I was for the first time playing in the series as a member of the Brooklyn Dodgers team. It was a history-making day. It would be the first time that a black man would be allowed to participate in a world series. I had become the first black player in the major leagues.

—Jackie Robinson,
I Never Had It Made, 1972

I like Ike.

—Campaign slogan
for Dwight Eisenhower, 1952

I keep picturing all these little kids in this big field of rye. . . . If they're running and they don't look where they're going I have to come out from somewhere and catch them. That's all I'd do all day. I'd just be the catcher in the rye and all. I know it's crazy.

—J. D. Salinger,
The Catcher in the Rye, 1951

First fight. Then fiddle.
Win war. Rise bloody, maybe not too late
For having first to civilize a space
Wherein to play your violin with grace.

—Gwendolyn Brooks,
Annie Allen, 1949

Don't put a cold in your pocket!—
Use **Kleenex** Tissues.

—Kleenex ad, 1951

George: Gracie, what do you think of television?

Gracie: I think it's wonderful—I hardly watch radio anymore.

—Joke told on TV's
The George Burns and Gracie Allen Show, 1950

The more people have studied different methods of bringing up children the more they have come to the conclusion that what good mothers and fathers instinctively feel like doing for their babies is the best after all.

—Benjamin Spock,
*The Common Sense Book
of Baby and Child Care,* 1946

"*Every intellectual who is called before one of the committees ought to refuse to testify, i.e., he must be prepared . . . for the sacrifice of his personal welfare in the interest of the cultural welfare of his country. . . . This kind of inquisition violates the spirit of the Constitution.*"

—Albert Einstein, 1953

"*One of these days, Alice. One of these days—POW!—right to the moon!*"

—Jackie Gleason in
The Honeymooners, 1955–1956

JAMES DEAN, FILM ACTOR, KILLED IN CRASH OF AUTO

—New York Times, October 1, 1955

You ain't nothin' but a hound dog,
Cryin' all the time.
You ain't nothin' but a hound dog,
Cryin' all the time.
Well, you ain't never caught a rabbit
And you ain't no friend of mine.

—Jerry Leiber and Mike Stoller,
"Hound Dog," 1956

"*You don't understand. I could have had class. I could have been a contender. I could have been somebody—instead of a bum, which is what I am, let's face it.*"

—Marlon Brando in the film
On the Waterfront, 1954

Who's the leader of the club
that's made for you and me?
M-I-C-K-E-Y M-O-U-S-E!

—Jimmie Dodd,
"Mickey Mouse March," 1958

The sea lies all about us. The commerce of all lands must cross it. The very winds that move over the lands have been cradled on its broad expanse and seek ever to return to it. The continents themselves dissolve and pass to the sea, in grain after grain of eroded land. So the rains that rose from it return again in rivers. In its mysterious past it encompasses all the dim origins of life and receives in the end, after, it may be, many transmutations, the dead husks of that same life. For all at last returns to the sea—to Oceanus, the ocean river, like the ever-flowing stream of time, the beginning and the end.

—Rachel Carson, The Sea Around Us, 1951

*T*he buck stops here.

—Harry S. Truman, 1955

"*Democracy cannot be saved by supermen, but only by the unswerving devotion and goodness of millions of little men.*"

—Adlai Stevenson, 1955

RUSSIANS ANNOUNCE FIRING INTERCONTINENTAL MISSILE 'HUGE DISTANCE' TO TARGET

—*New York Times, August 27, 1957*

Cigarette Smoking Linked To Cancer in High Degree

American Society Makes Final Report on Study of 187,783 Men—Industry Disputes Statistical Studies

—*New York Times, June 5, 1957*

I saw the best minds of my generation destroyed by madness,
    starving hysterical naked,
dragging themselves through the negro streets at dawn looking for
    an angry fix
angelheaded hipsters burning for the ancient heavenly connection
    to the starry dynamo in the machinery of night.

—Allen Ginsberg, *Howl*, 1956

The sun did not shine
It was too wet to play.
So we sat in the house
All that cold, cold, wet day.
We looked!
Then we saw him step in on the mat!
We looked!
And we saw him!
The Cat in the Hat!

—Dr. Seuss,
The Cat in the Hat, 1957

SOVIET FIRES NEW SATELLITE, CARRYING DOG

—*New York Times, November 3, 1957*

Winstons taste good
like a cigarette should.

—Winston cigarettes ad, 1957

"*I*n the councils of government, we must guard against the acquisition of unwarranted influence, whether sought or unsought, by the military-industrial complex. The potential for the disastrous rise of misplaced power exists and will persist."

—Dwight D. Eisenhower, 1961

"*T*he New Frontier of which I speak is not a set of promises—it is a set of challenges. It sums up not what I intend to offer the American people, but what I intend to ask of them."

—John F. Kennedy, 1960

PRESIDENT SENDS TROOPS TO LITTLE ROCK

—*New York Times, September 25, 1957*

VOICES OF THE ERA

"*I have a dream that my four little children will one day live in a nation where they will not be judged by the color of their skin, but by the content of their character.*"

—Martin Luther King Jr., 1963

"*Whatever women do they must do twice as well as men to be thought half as good. Luckily, this is not difficult.*"

—Charlotte Whitton, 1963

Who knows what women can be when they are finally free to become themselves? Who knows what women's intelligence will contribute when it can be nourished without denying love? . . . The time is at hand when the voices of the feminine mystique can no longer drown out the inner voice that is driving women on to become complete.

—Betty Friedan,
The Feminine Mystique, 1963

Willy was a salesman. And for a salesman, there is no rock bottom to the life. He don't put a bolt to a nut, he don't tell you the law or give you medicine. He's a man way out there in the blue, riding on a smile and a shoeshine. And when they start not smiling back—that's an earthquake. And then you get yourself a couple of spots on your hat, and you're finished. Nobody dast blame this man. A salesman is got to dream, boy. It comes with the territory.

—Arthur Miller,
Death of a Salesman, 1962

KENNEDY IS KILLED BY SNIPER AS HE RIDES IN CAR IN DALLAS; JOHNSON SWORN IN ON PLANE

—*New York Times,* November 23, 1963

"*I draw the line in the dust and toss the gauntlet before the feet of tyranny and I say segregation now, segregation tomorrow, segregation forever.*"

—George Wallace,
inaugural address, 1963

Well, I've got a hammer, and I've got a bell,
And I've got a song, All over this land,
It's the hammer of justice, it's the bell of freedom,
It's the song about love between my brothers and my sisters
All over this land.

—Lee Hays and Pete Seeger,
"If I Had a Hammer," 1958

Come alive!
You're in the **Pepsi** generation.

—Pepsi ad, 1963

Glossary

Allies: during World War II, the countries that fought against Germany, Italy, and Japan, including the United Kingdom, the USSR, and the United States

annexation: the process of incorporating new territory into an existing state or country

antibiotic: a drug that fights and destroys bacterial infections and is widely used to treat and prevent diseases

apartheid: a government policy of racial segregation in South Africa

arms race: competition among nations in accumulating weapons

avant-garde: the leaders in new or unconventional movements, especially in the arts

Axis: during World War II, the countries (including Germany, Japan, and Italy) that fought against the Allies

blacklist: a list of persons or organizations that are disapproved of, punished, or banned

capitalism: an economic system controlled by individuals and corporations rather than by government, characterized by open competition in a free market

coalition: a working union of parties, persons, or governments, which usually has a specific goal or purpose

containment: the policy of preventing a hostile country from expanding its influence

de facto segregation: separation of races as a result of where people live, as opposed to segregation as a result of law

diversify: to increase variety

epidemic: the rapid spread of a contagious disease

existentialist: relating to the philosophy that emphasizes that the individual is responsible for his or her own actions and can determine his or her destiny

fallout: airborne radioactive particles that result from a nuclear explosion

fascism: a government system in which an extreme right-wing dictatorship controls a nation

food chain: an arrangement of a series of organisms in which each eats a smaller one and is, in turn, eaten by a larger one

franchise: the right to own a member team as granted by a league in certain professional sports

genetics: the scientific study of heredity

ghetto: a poor section of a city occupied by a specific racial or ethnic group

gross national product: the total dollar value of all the goods and services produced in a country in one year

guerrillas: a small, independent band of people who fight as part of a patriotic or revolutionary movement

Holocaust: the mass murder of more than 6 million Jews by the Nazis during World War II

imperialism: the domination of one nation over others by acquiring territories or controlling a nation's political or economic life

inflation: a general increase in prices and fall in the purchasing value of money in an economy

minimalist: in art, referring to the practice of reducing to essential elements in order to maximize the effect

mobilization: the process of assembling troops for war

multinational: operating in two or more countries

nationalist: one who is devoted to the interests of a nation

nationalize: to transfer ownership of land and property from private owners to the government

nuclear fission: the splitting of the nucleus of an atom, resulting in the release of large amounts of energy

poll taxes: taxes formerly levied on every adult as a requirement for voting

prejudice: an unreasonable hatred or distrust of people belonging to a particular race, religion, or group

propaganda: material intended to spread information and ideas that influence people's opinions

protectorate: government by a strong nation that protects and partially controls a weak one

racism: the belief that one race is superior to other races

realism: representing things in art and literature as they are in reality

recession: a temporary decline in economic activity

sit-in: a form of nonviolent protest in which people sit in chairs or on the floor of a racially segregated establishment

socialism: an economic theory that promotes governmental control of factories and other businesses

social welfare program: a program established to help specific groups, such as the elderly or the unemployed

subsidy: a grant or gift of money

subsidizing: supporting financially with a grant or gift

summit: a meeting between the heads of two or more governments

telecommunications: methods of communication by electronic transmission of impulses, as by telegraph, cable, radio, or television

Third World: the underdeveloped countries of Asia, Africa, and Latin America

unconstitutional: not in accordance with a particular constitution

urbanization: the process of changing a place into a citylike area

welfare state: a social system in which the state assumes responsibility for the social welfare of its citizens

Zionism: a movement founded by the Jewish people to establish a homeland in Palestine

Suggested Readings

General

Abbott, Carl. *Urban America in the Modern Age, 1920 to Present.* H. Davidson, 1987.

Allen, Frederick Lewis. *The Big Change, 1900–1950.* Bantam, 1965.

Blum, Daniel. *A Pictorial History of the Silent Screen.* Grosset & Dunlap, 1953.

Cairns, Trevor. *The Twentieth Century.* Cambridge University Press, 1984.

Cantor, Norman F., and Michael S. Werthman, eds. *The History of Popular Culture.* Macmillan, 1968.

Churchill, Allen. *The Great White Way.* E. P. Dutton, 1962.

Daniels, Roger. *Coming to America: A History of Immigration and Ethnicity in American Life.* HarperCollins, 1990.

Davids, Jules. *America and the World of Our Time.* Random House, 1960.

Ewing, Elizabeth. *History of Twentieth Century Fashion.* Barnes & Noble, 1986.

Filene, Peter G. *Him/Her/Self: Sex Roles in Modern America.* Johns Hopkins University Press, 1986.

Flink, James J. *The Automobile Age.* MIT, 1988.

Freidel, Frank. *America in the Twentieth Century.* Knopf, 1960.

Goff, Richard. *The Twentieth Century: A Brief Global History.* John Wiley, 1983.

Hine, Darlene Clark, ed. *Black Women in American History.* Carlson Publishing, 1990.

Manchester, William. *The Glory and the Dream: A Narrative History of America, 1932–1972.* Little, Brown, 1974.

May, George S., ed. *The Automobile Industry, 1920–1980.* Facts on File, 1989.

Morgan, Robert P. *Twentieth-Century Music: A History of Musical Style in Modern Europe and America.* Norton, 1991.

Noble, David W., David A. Horowitz, and Peter N. Carroll. *Twentieth Century Limited: A History of Recent America.* Houghton Mifflin, 1980.

Norman, Philip. *The Road Goes On Forever: Portraits from a Journey Through Contemporary Music.* Simon & Schuster, 1982.

Olderman, Murray. *Nelson's Twentieth Century Encyclopedia of Baseball.* Nelson, 1963.

Oliver, John W. *History of American Technology.* Books on Demand UMI, 1956.

Ritter, Lawrence S. *The Story of Baseball.* Morrow, 1983.

Sklar, Robert. *Movie-Made America: A Cultural History of American Movies.* Random House, 1976.

Spaeth, Sigmund. *A History of Popular Music in America.* Random House, 1948.

Susman, Warren I. *Culture as History: The Transformation of American Society in the Twentieth Century.* Pantheon, 1984.

Taft, Philip. *Organized Labor in American History.* Harper & Row, 1964.

Vecsey, George, ed. *The Way It Was: Great Sports Events from the Past.* McGraw-Hill, 1974.

Zinn, Howard. *The Twentieth Century: A People's History.* Harper & Row, 1984.

About the Era

Carson, Rachel Louise. *Silent Spring.* Houghton Mifflin, 1962.

Carter, Paul A. *Another Part of the Fifties.* Columbia University Press, 1983.

Gitlin, Todd. *The Sixties.* Bantam, 1989.

Goldman, Eric F. *The Crucial Decade and After: America, 1945–1960.* Random House, 1960.

Harrington, Michael. *The Other America: Poverty in the United States.* Viking Penguin, 1971.

Hendler, Herb. *Year by Year in the Rock Era: Events and Conditions Shaping the Rock Generations That Reshaped America.* Greenwood, 1983.

Jezer, Marty. *The Dark Ages: Life in the United States, 1945–1960.* South End, 1982.

Leuchtenberg, William E. *The Age of Change: From 1945.* Silver Burdett, 1974.

Lewis, David L. *King: A Biography,* 2nd ed. University of Illinois Press, 1978.

Lindop, Edmund. *An Album of the Fifties.* Franklin Watts, 1978.

Lowe, Jacques. *Kennedy: A Time Remembered.* Quartet Books, 1983.

Mets, David R. *NATO: Alliance for Peace.* Messner, 1981.

Miller, Merle. *Plain Speaking: An Oral Biography of Harry S. Truman.* Berkley Books, 1986.

Nader, Ralph. *Unsafe at Any Speed.* Pocket Books, 1965, 1966.

O'Neill, William L. *Coming Apart: An Informal History of the 1960s.* Random House, 1974.

Perett, Geoffrey. *A Dream of Greatness: The American People, 1945–1963.* Coward, McCann & Geoghegan, 1979.

Reeves, Thomas C. *The Life and Times of Joe McCarthy: A Biography.* Stein and Day, 1982.

Schlesinger, Arthur M., Jr. *A Thousand Days: John F. Kennedy in the White House.* Fawcett, 1977.

Truman, Margaret. *Harry S Truman.* Morrow, 1984.

White, Theodore H. *The Making of the President, 1960.* Atheneum, 1961.

Wright, Lawrence. *In the New World: Growing Up with America from the Sixties to the Eighties.* Random House, 1989.

Index